MME DE VILLEDIEU'S LES DÉSORDRES DE L'AMOUR

History, Literature, and the **Nouvelle Historique**

Arthur Flannigan

UNIVERSITY
PRESS OF
AMERICA

Copyright © 1982 by

University Press of America, Inc.

P.O. Box 19101, Washington, D.C. 20036

Printed in the United States of America

ISBN (Perfect): 0-8191-2697-7
ISBN   (Cloth): 0-8191-2696-9

Library of Congress Catalog Card Number: 82-43835

Parts of this study were first presented in dissertation form to the Department of Romance Languages of the Johns Hopkins University in 1978. All sections have since been edited and revised in an effort to render the whole more easily accessible to the student of French literature-- the non-specialist and the specialist alike.

A. F.
Los Angeles, 1980

TABLE OF CONTENTS

INTRODUCTION

Madame de Villedieu was perhaps one of the first women in France whose very subsistence depended often on her literary productions alone; at times during her career she had no other means of support. She was born Marie-Catherine Desjardins in Alençon around 1632. Very little is known about her education and formation; in fact, very little is known about her life at all until she began publishing her works. Her career, which spans the years between 1662 and 1675, parallels that part of the seventeenth century that fashioned what subsequently has been esteemed as many of the "greatest" productions of the Classical period. She had at least some contact with many of the notable personalities of the period. She was, with the famous Madeleine de Scrudéry, in fact one of only two women writers to be pensioned by Louis XIV himself.[1]

Moreover, during this period of such fertile, fervent, and normative literary production and consumption, few writers enjoyed a popularity comparable to hers. This popularity--evident in part by the numerous editions of her individual and collected works--seems to have persisted well into the eighteenth century; and the nineteenth witnessed the formation of a cult of her admirers.[2] Her works cover the entire gamut of Classical genres: poetry, ballets, (pseudo-) memoirs, letters, nouvelles, comedy and tragedy; and though she was considered by some literary historians of her century, and remains for those of ours, a "minor" author, her works, by virtue of sheer volume and diversity alone, demand at least some critical attention. For even if one were to conclude that Mme de Villedieu's *oeuvre* exhibits no unusual literary value, it would still not warrant total critical neglect by the student of seventeenth-century literature, since the universally acclaimed "great" and "ingenious" works of the Classical period constitute but a small part of what was produced and consumed during the epoch. It has been suggested elsewhere even that her enormously popular works more accurately reflect the reading public than those of the more acclaimed authors, for they obviously offered what was desired and demanded of a "good" writer.[3]

1

Any author judged as "minor" (*vis-à-vis* his or her contemporaries esteemed as "major") is invariably condemned to a position of inferiority. Thus Mme de Villedieu's plays are dismissed in light of Corneille's; her fables are found to be "weak and inferior" when placed next to those of La Fontaine; and her letters are considered "lacking" when compared to those of Mme de Sévigné, etc.-- and perhaps not unjustly. Of more than three hundred poems, eight fables, three plays, and about twenty nouvelles or novels, only one of this prolific author's works has attained any kind of notoriety--*Les Désordres de l'Amour*, first published in 1675. And indeed it is undeniably with her nouvelles and with this text in particular that Mme de Villedieu has left her indelible mark in French literary history. This text appears on the surface to be a collection of four nouvelles interspersed with aphoristic poetry; but, as the present study will demonstrate, it is not a question of *four* separate or independent stories nor is it a question of a collection in the usual sense of the word.

Furthermore, of the four parts that comprise *Les Désordres de l'Amour*, one section alone has attacted the attention of critics; and even this has been in a very limited manner. First of all, this particular part of the text has never constituted the object of any systematic and serious study; and, secondly, it has never been examined or even cited in and for itself. Indeed, this nouvelle has received critical attention only insofar as it can be linked to *La Princesse de Clèves*--for which it did or did not serve as a model, depending upon the particular critic. This comparison, which began in 1678 with Valincourt (*Lettres à la Marquise sur le sujet de la Princesse de Clèves*) and continues with Roger Francillon in 1975 (*L'Oeuvre Romanesque de Mme de Lafayette*), has become a *lieu commun* and indeed a necessary part of any study on seventeenth-century prose.[4]

As it is uniquely in its relationship to Mme de Lafayette's text that *Les Désordres de l'Amour* is familiar to the present-day reader, it would perhaps not be inappropriate to recall briefly the circumstances surrounding their publications.

La Princesse de Clèves first appeared in March, 1678 and it was immediately successful due in large part to the now-famous confession scene. The newspaper *Le Mercure Galant* even conducted a poll to determine whether or not Mme de Clèves was "justified" in making such a confession. A few months later Valincourt wrote the anonymous *Lettres* which created a veritable stir. He revealed that it was not the author of *La Princesse de Clèves* who had invented the confession scene but the author of *Les Désordres de l'Amour*. It was the abbé de Charnes who responded that the author of *La Princesse de Clèves* had for a long time before its publication date thought out and developed her plot. This affirmation prompted some critics to propose that it was perhaps Mme de Villedieu who profited from an earlier manuscript of Mme de Lafayette. There was some doubt that *Les Désordres de l'Amour* actually antedated Mme de Lafayette's novel: there is, for example, an indication by the publisher Barbin in 1671 of a "Prince de Clèves" that was to appear-- it never did. There is equally in a 1672 letter by Mme de Sévigné a reference to a "Princesse de Clèves"; but another letter in March of 1678 indicates that the novel had just appeared--*Lettres de Mme de Sévigné,* ed. Gérard-Gailly, II, 424, 462).

Presently, there is no doubt that Les *Désordres de l'Amour* antedates *La Princesse de Clèves*. Concerning the contention that Mme de Villedieu could have used an earlier manuscript of Mme de Lafayette, Roger Francillon (who examines the construction of both works) demonstrates the extreme improbability of this claim. Upon close examination, it is clear that the two confessions are quite different. Mme de Termes is a devastated woman whose confession, unlike that of Mme de Clèves, has no heroic implications. Moreover, the consequences of the confessions differ: M. de Termes, unlike his counterpart in Mme de Lafayette's novel, is not torn and destroyed by jealousy and even sanctions his wife's marriage to her lover. In the final analysis, the princesse de Clèves is left alone after her husband's death and has to suppress her passion; Mme de Termes "experiences" her passion to its tragic conclusions. And it is precisely this experience of passion which Mme de Clèves denies herself that

3

constitutes the subject proper of Mme de Villedieu's text.

There exists, to my knowledge, but three studies devoted exclusively to Mme de Villedieu (the most recent dating back to the 1940's); and they consist principally of biographies of the writer or catalogues of her publications.[5] Elsewhere, there are brief references or occasionally a few paragraphs devoted to her but she is unequivocally dismissed as "mineure," and her other works, including the remaining nouvelles of *Les Désordres de l'Amour,* are described as "mal écrites," "fort médiocres," "sans intérêt," etc. This is true, for example, in one of the few modern works where some mention is made of this text. In his otherwise excellent study of *La Princesse de Clèves* and the *romanesque* productions of the seventeenth century in general, Roger Francillon dismisses with a few phrases all of the other prose of Mme de Villedieu. And as for *Les Désordres de l'Amour,* he quickly dismisses the first, third and fourth parts of this text as totally devoid of interest; he then proceeds to consider the second uniquely in light of the claim that Mme de Lafayette used it as a model. He writes of Mme de Villedieu and her text:

> Son ouvrage se présente sous la forme de quatre parties qui constituent quatre nouvelles différentes dont l'action se situe. . . comme celle de Mme de Lafayette au XVIe siècle. Nous ne retiendrons que la deuxième de ces histoires, celle qui fait l'objet du litige. . . (p. 270)

Curiously enough, although many critics refer to *Les Désordres de l'Amour,* until very recently there has not even been an easily accessible edition of the text in print. Until the 1970 edition in the series *Textes Littéraires Françaises* (Droz), the latest edition was the 1770 copy found in a collection of the author's work.[6] It is my present intention to undertake a careful and systematic study of this text. As much criticism can be aimed at its seemingly "rambling" and "disjointed" nature, I shall address myself especially to the question of the internal coherence or lack thereof of *Les Désordres de l'Amour.*

4

The assigning of such a pivileged position to this particular text in the author's long list of works demands perhaps further justification insofar as my present comments are concerned. This "position," I hope, will be legitimized and rendered evident during the course of the study itself. I shall be content here to affirm that *Les Désordres de l'Amour* is the last work to have been published during the author's lifetime and that it constitutes the pinnacle of an evolution that had its gestation in the very first nouvelle written by the author--begun when Marie-Catherine had barely attained her sixteenth year--*Alcidamie* (1661)[7]. The implication here, of course, is that *Les Désordres de l'Amour* does not constitute an absolutely unique artistic form. It shares certain aspects with other works by Mme de Villedieu as well as with works by other authors. Thus it can be seen as part of an opus and as part of a "movement." Hence, the illumination of this text will not only afford further perception and appreciation of Mme de Villedieu and her prose productions but it will provide equally valuable insight into the *nouvelle historique* as a Classical genre (in which she so excelled) and further elucidation of the entire literary movement in which she unquestionably occupies an important position.

Yet the principal preoccupation of this study will hardly result in the comparison of Mme de Villedieu to other writers; nor will it result essentially in the comparison of *Les Désordres de l'Amour* to her other nouvelles. My focus will center on this text itself as I shall be concerned foremost with how it theorizes about its own artistic form and production. And if the form of this Classical text is to constitute the center of attention, then one essentially implicit question will underlie my observations: how does the author proceed in *selecting* and *organizing* her materials. Consequently, this study may appear at times to be somewhat overburdened by a virtual line-by-line analysis of the text; yet, though this kind of close examination may not always be the easiest to read, it is perhaps the best way to proceed when confronting a relatively unknown text such as this. For it is when this selection and arrangement of materials, from the most specific to the most general, can be accounted for that I shall be able to define and specify the textuality and signification of *Les Désordres de l'Amour*.

A careful reading of this text suggests that its author, in constructing and in developing her plots, adheres closely to the historical documents of the seventeenth century. By embedding a historical *énoncé* into her nouvelles, Mme de Villedieu has, from a critical perspective, inscribed her text in a curiously illuminating sphere. *Les Désordres de l'Amour* appears to be a text that periodically and almost instantaneously "shifts" from the discursive to the narrative mode, from *récit historique* to *discours*.[8]   A historical text, in other words, provides the skeleton for the nouvelles; and the text--which, as I shall attempt to show, is indeed itself intimately "historical"--is one that allows me to examine the relationship between and the passage from *énoncé* (the historical event) to *énonciation* (the literary event or activity): that is to say, the conditions under which this transformation takes place and the consequences of the collision of these two times--the time of the event (history), the time of its evocation (literature).[9]   This 1675 text permits one to identify these points of passage, these moments or "instances" that can be characterized in effect as the eruption of a *discours* within the fabric of a *récit*. In terms of the Classical esthetics at least, it allows one, therefore, to witness the process whereby history becomes literature.

I shall then be concerned here first with history in Mme de Villedieu's nouvelles. The first part of this study will propose an account of what materials are selected from the historical documents and how they are chosen. Secondly, I shall be concerned here with literature; the second part of this study will examine the form and degree of the representation of the events of history which makes *Les Désordres de l'Amour*, in a Classical perspective, literature and not history. Finally, in the third part of this study, I shall be concerned with the birth and the textuality of the genre that we know as the *nouvelle historique*.

6

NOTES

INTRODUCTION

1. Bruce Morrissette, *The Life and Works of Marie-Catherine Desjardins (Mme de Villedieu), 1632-1683* (St. Louis: Washington University Press, 1947), vii.

2. Daniel Mornet, "Les Enseignements des Bibliothèques Privées, 1750-1780," *Revue d'Histoire Littéraire de la France,* (1910), p. 473; and M. Chavardès, *Histoire de la Librairie en France* (Paris: Waleffe, 1967).

3. Mme de Villedieu, *Les Désordres de l'Amour,* ed. Micheline Cuénin (Paris: Droz, 1970).

4. The interval between Valincourt and Francillon is comprised of the following works:

   Abbé de Charnes, *Conversations sur la critique de la Princesse de Clèves* (Paris: Barbin, 1679)

   A. Praviel, "Madame de Villedieu et *la Princesse de Clèves,"* *Revue Littéraire,* (1899)

   Henri Chatenet, *Le Roman et les Romans d'une Femme de Lettres au XVIIe Siècle: Madame de Villedieu* (Paris: Champion, 1911)

   H. Ashton, *Mme de Lafayette* (Cambridge: University Press, 1922), p. 163.

   André Beaunier, *L'Amie de la Rochefoucauld* (Paris: Flammarion, 1927)

   M. Aline Raynal, *Le Talent de Madame de Lafayette* (Paris: Picart, 1927, p. 235.

   D. Dallas, *Le Roman Français de 1660-1685* (Paris: Gamber, 1932), p. 191.

9

B. Morrissette, *The Life and Works of Marie-Catherine Desjardins*, 1947

Henri Coulet, *Le Roman Français jusqu'à la Révolution*, Collection U (Paris: Armand Colin, 1967), t. 1., p. 226.

5. These are Henri Chatenet, *Madame de Villedieu*, 1911; E. Magne, *Mme de Villedieu*, 1907; B. Morrissette, *The Life and Works of Marie-Catherine Desjardins*, 1947. It has come to my attention at the time of this writing, however, that Micheline Cuénin is about to publish her thesis (in French) on Madame de Villedieu. It is not yet available.

6. I am referring, of course, to the Cuénin edition cited above.

7. This has been adequately and convincingly demonstrated by Morrissette (Chapter V: "Historical Novels and Nouvelles").

8. It is Emile Benveniste in *Problèmes de Linguistique Générale* (Paris: Gallimard (NRF), 1966) who delineates these two distinct and complementary systems into which the tenses of (French) verbs are organized. These two systems are manifest in two levels of utterances (*énonciations*): *histoire* and *discours*.

The historical utterance characterizes the relation of *past events*. It presents facts (that occurred at some point in the past) without the intervention of the speaker into the relation. Thus the *récit historique* excludes any linguistic form associated with "autobiography." If strictly followed, one would find only forms of the third person in such a *récit*. There would be no reflections, no comparisons--in effect, as Benveniste writes, no narrator: "Les événements sont posés comme ils se sont produits; personne ne parle ici; les événements semblent se raconter eux-mêmes." The fundamental tense of the *récit historique* is the aorist (passé simple): the present tense is excluded for it would necessarily constitute the present of the historian.

Benveniste defines *discours*, conversely, as any

utterance supposing a speaker and a listener and the intention on the part of the first to somehow or in some way influence the second. The *discours* avails itself then of all the personal forms of the verb including the *je/tu* configuration.

I have opted to keep the French terms "récit historique" and discours," etc. rather than their English or American equivalents for the sake of clarity and consistency.

9. It is Roman Jakobson who has distinguished between speech event *(énonciation)* and narrated event *(énoncé)*:

> In order to classify the verbal categories two basic distinctions are to be observed:
>
> 1) speech itself (s), and its topic, the narrated matter (n);
>
> 2) the event itself (E), and any of its participants (P), whether 'performer' or 'undergoer'.
>
> Consequently four items are to be distinguished: a narrated event (En), a speech event (Es), a participant of the narrated event (Pn), a participant of the speech event (Ps), whether addresser or addressee.
>
> Any verb is concerned with a narrated event. Verbal categories may be subdivided into those which do and those which do not involve the participants of the event. These categories then . . .may characterize the narrated event *(procès de l'énoncé)* and/or its participants either without or with reference to the speech event *(procès de l'énonciation)* or its participants. Categories implying such a reference are to be termed SHIFTERS; those without such a reference are NON-SHIFTERS.
>
> ("Shifters, Verbal Categories, and the Russian Verb," in *Selected Writings*, II (Paris: Mouton, 1971), pp. 130-147.

PART I
THE HISTORICAL EVENT
(ÉNONCÉ)

CHAPTER ONE

A "MEETING" WITH MÉZERAY[1]

Les Désordres de l'Amour quite obviously belongs to that literary corpus known as the *nouvelle historique*--a genre whose very denomination attests to a certain ambiguity in its nature. The curious juxtaposition of these two terms, "nouvelle" and "historique," already suggests perhaps some kind of confusion: Is it history that has been fictionalized; or, rather, is it fiction that has become historicized? What might be the exact nature of this rapport? Simply rephrased, what is the role and status of history in the Classical nouvelle?[2]

Even for that reader not particularly well-versed in the specifics of French history, a reading of *Les Désordres de l'Amour* would give the impression that this is a historical account. This is not to say that the text contains a proliferation of dates or a "litany" of the succession of monarchs. On the contrary, it contains very little of this; it is rather the names of the principal characters (Henri III, Catherine de Medici, the duc de Guise, etc.) and references to certain sixteenth-century events that tend to anchor these nouvelles into a precise historical context. The question perhaps inevitably arises as to which historian(s) served as possible source(s) for this writer of literature. Textual evidence tends to point to one name in particular: François Eudes de Mézeray. There are, of course, other possible sources; but it appears that Mme de Villedieu exploits them somewhat sparingly, obtaining a name here, a small detail there.[3] On the whole, then, Mézeray is her guide and she follows him faithfully.

An examination of Mézeray's *Histoire de France* suggests that Mme de Villedieu is indebted to this early seventeenth-century historian for two things: the general chronology of the plots of her nouvelles and certain psychological traits that serve to stimulate her imagination. The materials that Mézeray uses and "organizes" as historian, she "recycles" as novelist/moralist. This "meeting" of the historian and the moralist at a historical moment when their projects were so similar can perhaps help to illuminate the activity of each. For my present purposes, I shall use it to examine further the artistic imagination of the novelist. Moreover, this "meeting," I postulate, will serve to clarify some of the theoretical implications of the *nouvelle historique*, thereby allowing me to propose some hypotheses as to the nature of this Classical genre.

To this end, a few brief but necessary observations are first in order: François Eudes de Mézeray began his own career as a poet. Later, as artillery officer of the royal forces, he conceived of a history of France that would differ somewhat from the existing histories. He proposed that it should conserve the memory of glorious events of the past while agreeably entertaining the reader. With the support of Richelieu, he ventured to realize his project. And the project of the historian, as Mézeray embarked upon it, was essentially to expose the motives of princes that form and influence political life. Mézeray concentrated his efforts on sixteenth-century France during the upheaval of the religious wars where the infiltration of personal motives into politics appears to have been particularly apparent. But, as this present study will subsequently establish, the exploitation of these personal motives constituted the domain proper of fiction. Already, one can sense the curious interpenetration of the nouvelle and history.

In effect, the difference between a Mézeray and a Villedieu is, in some respects, quite negligible. The ultimate goal of each is to instruct. This seventeenth-century historian who, unlike his contemporary counterpart, seems at times unconcerned about or indifferent towards sources or documentation, is concerned (as is the novelist) with the motives and the psychology of history's principal actors.[4] He is most concerned, however, with what constitutes the political reality: wars, treaties, court events, etc., and seems to have formulated as his goal the penetration into

16

the secret royal councils to reveal their resolutions and to indicate their faults and fallacies.
It is in this way that history was to be used as a
political guide for future princes and their
ministers.[5]

This lack of rigorous documentation not-
withstanding, there is little doubt that Mme de
Villedieu read Mézeray as *Histoire*, that is to
say, as *vérité*. In the composition of her
nouvelles, Mme de Villedieu, by respecting what
she considered to be the important established
facts and trends in history (she writes in her
first nouvelle of "les vérités importantes de
l'histoire générale"), could still invest or
enlarge the historical account with scenes of
amorous intrigues to make it above all else a
viable moral guide for everyone. And there is
equally little doubt that this novelist identified
her own undertaking with that of the historian.

Moreover, since in the seventeenth century
the historian and the novelist (in general) shared
not only the same materials and the same general
aims but since they both also subscribed to similar esthetic rules, one might ask what are the
factors which make *Les Désordres de l'Amour*, in a
Classical perspective, a nouvelle and not history;
or, in other words, how is the Classical *nouvelle
historique* to be extricated from the *Histoire*.[6]

One could begin quite logically indeed by
examining the role or status of history in these
nouvelles by Mme de Villedieu. One can perhaps
simplify the matter by stating somewhat naively
that what the novelist extracts from the historical account can be divided into two broad
categories: subjects (le prince, le roi, la
marquise, etc.) and predicates (faire siège, faire
la guerre, négocier la paix, etc.): that is to
say, a general atmosphere, characters, and events.
Overall, the novelist faithfully and meticulously
respects the background and the facts of history
as she read and understood them. Her nouvelles
begin with the ascension of Henri III to the
throne. Political and military activity in the
nouvelles, such as battles, treaties, sieges, etc.
are real. But it is especially in her precisions
about the workings of the Valois Court with its

inner fighting for influence and favor that Mme de Villedieu finds her basis in history.

In her first nouvelle, for example, she follows the account in Mézeray step by step in recounting the activities and the schemes of Catherine de Medici and the events that precede Henri III's marriage. Mme de Villedieu adheres to "historical truth" when she suggests that the efforts of Catherine were designed to create a confrontation between Monsieur, the king's brother, and the King of Navarre so as to avoid the danger of their possible alliance which could have posed a menace to the kingdom.[7]

In the second story, the historical atmosphere and background with which she fashions her nouvelle are amazingly authentic. The main action here, minus the retrospective and anticipatory passages, can be dated from the fall of 1574 when Henri III arrived at Turin to the spring of 1575. The nouvelle's heroine, Marguerite de Saluces, married first to the Maréchal de Termes and then to his nephew, is somewhat famous for her extraordinary beauty.[8] The plot of the third and fourth nouvelles, the story of Anne d'Anglure, is likewise to be found in the annals of history. It begins with the assassination of Henri de Guise in 1588 and it concludes with the siege of Laon in July, 1595. These last two nouvelles follow-- again step by step--the historical account to document the emergence of the League.

The difference that separates a Villedieu from a Mézeray, one could speculate, is essentially a difference in degrees. I do not propose, however, a "comparative" study or a study of genealogy strictly speaking; but by simply superimposing the events and the actors with which Mme de Villedieu composes her nouvelles with these same events and characters as they appear in the historical account, I am able to accomplish, in theory at least, two things: first, by observing what Mme de Villedieu *selects* from her source, I can attempt to identify the mechanisms of her selection process; and having done this, I could then, by closely examining the nouvelles, attempt to ascertain how she *combines* and represents these elements textually--namely, her mechanisms of arrangement and representation.

In other words, prior to any consideration of the mode of representation of the historical materials in *Les Désordres de l'Amour*, the process of *énonciation*, I must first turn my attention to a more precise estimation of what materials are selected from history and how they are chosen--or, as I shall formulate it in the forthcoming pages, the deconstruction (*découpage*) of the historical event.

THE DECONSTRUCTION OF THE HISTORICAL EVENT

Nouvelle 1:

("From the Power of Politics to the Power of Passion")[9]

For the purposes of my analysis (and for reasons that will become evident herein), one might subtitle this nouvelle in the following manner: "From the Power of Politics to the Power of Passion." In the introduction of this first story, it is very evident that Mme de Villedieu follows very closely the path paved by the historical accounts.[10] Although the image that she presents of Henri III is quite different from the final one in history, it is nevertheless, not a true contradiction of it. It is merely partial and somewhat incomplete.

The first portrait of this monarch in the third volume of Mézeray's *Histoire de France* is indeed a negative one. The historian states that after the death of Charles IX, the French were reasonably apprehensive about his successor (Henri) who, capricious and resentful because of the treatment he had previously received, did not possess the force or vigor required to rule effectively; nor, continues Mézeray, did he have the counsel or the patience to acquire these virtues.[11] Yet, although the overall picture of Henri in Mézeray's account is that of a weak, fickle, and easily manipulated monarch, the historian does provide one brief glimpse of him from the "Catholic" perspective:

> As much as Henri's reign provoked apprehension on the part of the Huguenots, it held hope for the Catholics: The young monarch had experience and courage which made his authority forceful as well as sensitivity and kindness which tempered

21

the possible harshness of his rule.

(III, 33, translation mine)

Mme de Villedieu chooses to ignore, or at
least to underplay, all of the negative things
about Henri III that may have given cause for
alarm and pessimism, and selects rather this one
positive image with which to open her nouvelle.
This selection produces some very definite consequences for the structuration of her story.
Because she begins precisely on an optimistic
note, the political and personal disorders that
follow, contradicting somewhat the reader's initial expectations, appear that much more unaccep-
table, misplaced, and unnecessary as the nouvelle
suggests that Henri surely had the potential to
stabilize his tumultuous kingdom. This element of
distaste for and disappointment in the king's per-
formance would have been absent had the novelist
begun, as does Mézeray, with an indictment pro-
claiming the king to be naturally indisposed to
govern efficiently.

In the first part of the nouvelle as in the
introduction, Mme de Villedieu is very close to
Mézeray. Both concur that Henri entertained many
lovers. And although as the nouvelle progresses
Henri proves not to be the perfect monarch that is
at first suggested, he is still not quite the
weak, emasculated pawn that history projects. Mme
de Villedieu chooses not to present, as does
Mézeray, the "flux et reflux des passions de ce
prince" where one remarks "dans toute sa vie, que
ses amours et ses haines & ses appetits repre-
noient souvent un grand accroissement après une
grande diminution" (III, 3). The historical document details, for example, the following sequence
in the monarch's mistresses: Anne (a Polish princess) - the princesse de Condé - Mlle de Châteauneuf
- Louise de Vaudemont - (back to) Mlle de
Châteauneuf - Mlle d'Elbeuf until he ultimately
espouses Queen Louise. The novelist summarizes
this entire progression very quickly, failing
altogether to mention Anne and the second infatuation with Mlle de Châteauneuf. But more importantly, the novelist, *adds* the name of one mistress that history fails to substantiate: Mme de

22

Sauve.

Although Mézeray does not cite Mme de Sauve
specifically as the "tool" used by Catherine de
Medici to divert Henri's attention away from the
undesirable princesse de Condé, this is entirely
possible for he does confirm that Henri's marriage
to Louise takes place only through the instigation
and the intervention of the queen mother; but the
historian does not specify which woman she uses to
accomplish this. In attributing this to Mme de
Sauve, Mme de Villedieu writes not only what is
historically possible but also what is highly
probable; for it is known, again from Mézeray,
that Mme de Sauve, an astonishingly attractive
woman, was used by the queen mother for similar
purposes on other occasions (III, 1-32).
Moreover, history suggests that it was the duc de
Guise who had, in the final analysis, relieved the
king of his depression after the death of the
princesse de Condé; and given the peculiar relationship between the duc de Guise and Mme de Sauve
(history has him, prior to this occasion, employ-
ing his former mistress to seduce and sedate the
king's brother (Monsieur)—III, 1-33), Mme de
Sauve may very well have played a part in this
affair.

This deconstruction (or these small modifications) of history in this first part of the
nouvelle has two immediate results: it shifts the
center of attention away from the king and at the
same time it increases the importance of Mme de
Sauve. It is a shift from politics to passion; or
rather, from the power of the king to the "power"
of passion. Significantly, Mme de Sauve is, in
the nouvelle, the king's preferred mistress; for
she is not just one in his series of lovers, she
is the only one influential enough to comfort
Henri. Thus she comes to possess such a "power"
over the king ("un pouvoir si absolu," p. 8) that
the queen mother uses this influence to her own
political advantage.[12]

Now that the nouvelle has modulated into Mme
de Sauve's "story," in a manner of speaking, one
would perhaps expect a greater distance between it
and the historical document. Indeed, the plot by
Mlle de Châteauneuf, Mlle d'Elbeuf, the Queen of

Navarre (and later the duc de Guise) against Mme de Sauve appears on the surface to be pure fiction. But the motivations for such a plot are not, as indeed these women were, again according to Mézeray, all competing for Henri's favor. Here, as is often the case in *Les Désordres de l'Amour*, historical fact provides the basis for developments and expansions in the nouvelle that consequently are not gratuitous fiction. By "germinating" the "seeds" (provided by history) for this plot and by including the duc de Guise in the intrigue, Mme de Villedieu transforms, in fact, only what "generates" the historical events and not the actual events themselves.

In *Histoire de France*, for example, it is the queen mother and her politics that motivate the sequence of events; here, it is the duc de Guise's *jealousy* of Mme de Sauve. It is because of this passion that the duke will convince Mlle de Châteauneuf to persuade the King of Navarre to insult Mme de Sauve. It is this passion that makes possible the King of Navarre's love adventure with Mme de Sauve, etc. Similarly, the jealousy between Monsieur and Navarre in Mézeray's narrative is instigated by the queen mother for political purposes; whereas in the nouvelle this jealousy is provoked for personal reasons by the duc de Guise after the loss of his mistress. What constitutes a possible means in history becomes an end in the nouvelle.

In a like manner, what in history is the duke's attempt to influence Henri III through Queen Louise in order to advance his political ambitions is modulated in the nouvelle into his attempt to influence Henri primarily to discredit and to disgrace Mme de Sauve. To be sure, Mme de Villedieu's duke is only marginally political. In effect, one observes here that, in the movement from history to historical fiction (if indeed one can speak of this first nouvelle as fiction), the role of the queen mother decreases while that of the duc de Guise increases, once again, politics yields to passion.

Certainly, Mme de Villedieu appears once more to be entering the realm of pure fiction when she has Guise reconcile his differences with his former mistress. This, however, as the focal point of the nouvelle, is made possible (and necessary) solely because of the preceding shift in emphasis. In the remainder of this part of the nouvelle, the novelist follows closely the historian in the general articulations of his narrative and diverges only on a few essentially secondary details.[13]

The same is true for the second and third parts of this first nouvelle where Mme de Villedieu's "modifications" are minor, never violating "les vérités importantes de l'Histoire générale" and serving invariably to privilege the story of the duc de Guise and Mme de Sauve.[14] For example, Mézeray does not specify that Mme de Sauve accompanied the queen mother to Champigny; and he certainly does not suggest that she alone was responsible for the cease-fire there. It was probably, according to Mézeray, the Maréchal de Montmorency who persuaded Monsieur to grant a truce. This, however, still does not constitute pure fiction on the part of the novelist for we do learn from another historical source that Mme de Sauve was indeed a member of Catherine's entourage when she undertook this journey.[15]

Much in the same vein, Mme de Villedieu invents or rather "speculates" as to a strong enough reason for vengeance that would provoke the Queen of Navarre to undertake a vendetta against Mme de Sauve. Consequently, she uses the incident of the exile of a certain Mlle de Torigny, a confidante of the Queen of Navarre. Both *Histoire de France* and Marguerite de Valois' *Mémoires* date this incident as occuring much later when, out of anger, Henri III expels this young servant from the court. Although Marguerite seems to hold a certain Du Gaust (who does play a minor role in the nouvelle) and Mme de Sauve responsible for this, it was not the reason for the Queen of Navarre's vendetta.[16]

Nouvelle II:

("The Reign of Passion")[17]

If the role of the king in the first
nouvelle has been reduced from the central position that his Majesty occupies in *Histoire de
France,* the monarch has all but disappeared in
this second one. One might characterize and subtitle it therefore as the complete "Reign of
Passion." In fact, Henri III is mentioned only
twice and then merely to situate the events in
question (pp. 87, 97). The image of a weak ruler
is again avoided with this movement from politics
to passion that characterizes the nouvelle's
attempt to document historical disorders.

This nouvelle offers the negative image (in
the photographic sense) of the historical document. In Mézeray's narrative, it is inalterably
and unquestionably a chronicle of Henri's reign.
The events are presented in light of the king's
movements, his attitudes, and his actions and
reactions; and the Maréchal de Termes, Mme de
Termes, and the baron de Bellegarde are minor
characters, mentioned only insofar as they may
have directly or indirectly influenced the events
of Henri's tenure. Moreover, whereas for Mézeray,
Termes and Bellegarde are uniquely military
figures, i.e. their lives are presented principally in terms of their military campaigns, in
Mme de Villedieu's "record," their military
careers seem almost incidental. It is rather
their private lives that assume center stage.
Thus, what is parenthetical in history pulsates in
the literary account just as that which is secondary in the latter constitutes the heart of the
former.

Unlike in the first story in which the principal actors are fairly close to the king (his
mother, brother, sister, brother-in-law, and
mistress) and therefore where history would provide many details concerning their lives and activities, here the main characters, in terms of the

king's *champ de vision,* are incidental personalities and, quite logically, the historical
document should offer little information about
them.[18] And indeed information about the Termes
and the Bellegardes in the last two volumes of
Histoire de France is both sparse and sporadic.
One can catch glimpses of them only at those few
moments where their activities intersect with
those of the royal prerogatives. Consequently,
one would expect that the writer of literature
will have to resort to more extensive "inventions"
or "speculations" in order to expand the historical account.

Yet, after close examination, one discovers
that Mme de Villedieu again adheres closely to the
facts as presented by Mézeray; and in this
nouvelle too she respects the personalities of
the characters involved. There is little, if
indeed any, pure fiction; and the changes or
supplements that the novelist adds to history
invariably find their basis in "fact" and never
contradict nor seriously upset the rules of
historical casuality. Even the concept of the
intercepted letter, upon which the entire nouvelle
is predicated, is not specifically a purely nove-
listic invention on the part of Mme de
Villedieu.[19] Mézeray writes in the third volume
of his history, for example, that the duchesse de
Savoie knew of Damville's disgrace and the dangers
which threatened him by "une lettre révélatrice de
la Reine-Mère trouvée dans le lit du roi" (III,
3).

Although, in the final analysis, Mézeray
recounts very little about the sixteenth-century
M. de Termes, this personage is mentioned in volumes two and three of the historical narrative
where there is a brief reference to his death (II,
1016) and another pertaining to his will. Mme de
Villedieu follows history in recounting that the
Maréchal de Termes, commander of the "gens
d'armes," was married to the much younger
Marguerite de Saluces (II, 1482-1542). As novelist, however, she invents a series of scenes
designed to reveal the nature of their relationship and marriage.[20] Yet, even while
inventing, she paints the Maréchal as indeed
history suggests that he was--a highly moral and

27

courageous gentlemen (III, 892). Likewise, his
bride, in both history and the nouvelle, is young,
inexperienced, and extremely beautiful (III, 32),
so that Mme de Villedieu merely lends the couple
words that in essence dramatize the dominant
aspects of their characters and personalities.
Therefore, Mme de Termes' confession (as the
central scene in the first part of the nouvelle),
while pure fiction in terms of the actual words
spoken, is historical in terms of the sentiments
expressed: those of a young wife in love with her
husband's nephew.

Mme de Villedieu seems to depart from
history when she recounts that the Maréchal de
Termes was killed at the battle of Jarnac, an
altercation that took place on 13 March 1569. It
was a bloody and murderous confrontation that
claimed the lives of several important personages
including the prince de Condé, 1er de Bourbon.
Mézeray writes: "Cette bataille que quelques-uns
nomment de Bassac, les autres de Jarnac, se donna
le 13 mars. La perte qu'y fit la France fut plus
grande pour la qualité que pour le nombre de
morts" (II, 1060). Though the Maréchal died in
reality seven years prior to this battle (1562),
it is plausible that he could have been killed
here. By having Termes perish during this particular battle, the novelist, first, reinforces
the fact that the Maréchal was a heroic character;
and, secondly, she can suggest that his death
followed closely the discovery of his wife's
secret passion. Yet Mme de Villedieu does not
"rewrite" history in the sense that she is
altering the cause and effect relationship of some
important established fact. She suggests neither
that it was passion that precipitated the battle
of Jarnac nor that it was passion alone (or rather
unrequited love) that drove the Maréchal to an
untimely death.

Mme de Villedieu once again appears to be
deviating from historical fact when it is a
question in the nouvelle of the Maréchal's will.
According to Mézeray, he did leave his personal
wealth to his nephew: ". . .par faute d'enfans il
laissa la succession à Roger de Saint
Lary-Bellegarde, fils de sa soeur." (III, 892).
But nowhere is there mention of its specific con-

ditions. The stipulation that his nephew should marry his widow is in all likelihood Mme de Villedieu's addition. But as this is inspired from an old tradition of the nobility, the nouvelle consequently respects the rules of *vraisemblance* and at the same time avoids pure, gratuitous fiction.[21]

In addition to this, there are, in the first part of the second story, one or two occasions where Mme de Villedieu diverges from Mézeray on some minor point or where she adds some minor and seemingly incidental detail.[22] When, for example, she writes that Termes "étoit fort considéré du Roi Charles IX" (p. 68), this particular detail in *Histoire de France* applies to the nephew and not to the uncle:

> Ce seigneur avoit été assez bien auprès de Charles IX par l'entremise du Maréchal de Rais en recompense de ce qu'après la mort de Termes, son oncle, dont il avoit été lieutenant dans sa compagnie de gens d'armes, il s'étoit tant abaissé que de prendre la même charge dans celle de Rais, alors nouveau capitaine.

(III, 32)

And secondly, history does not substantiate that Mme de Termes' father, François de Saluces, intervened to prevent his daughter's marriage to Bellegarde. Though Mézeray does indeed state that the union was opposed, he does not specify who opposed it, qaulifying this opposition merely as "les reproches des honnestes gens" (III, 32). It is very likely, however, that the widow's father would indeed have been concerned about his daughter's reputation in this matter. Again, these changes are verisimilar and never violate or seriously contradict the important historical data.

In the last part of the story, Mme de Villedieu again differs from her source on a few essentially small points.[23] Roger de Saint-Lary de Bellegarde did in fact marry his uncle's widow in 1565; and, as Mézeray specifies, he did this "nonobstant les canons écclésiastiques & les reproches des honnestes gens" (III, 32). Moreover, Bellegarde did prove to be less than the perfect husband for "aussi-tost il la traita si mal qu'il laissa toujours à douter s'il la tenoit pour légitime" (III, 32). Mme de Villedieu follows the historian closely in reconstructing the difficulties that their marriage plans proposed for the young lovers as well as the accusations of kidnapping that were alleged (Mézeray, III, 32). She merely fills in the *gaps* of history by making a resentful and remorseful wife sabotage the career of her military husband.

One reads in Mézeray, as one does in the nouvelle, that Bellegarde was allied with the duc de Savoie; but whereas in history this friendship is the consequence of pure ambition on the part of an opportunistic Bellegarde, in *Les Désordres de l'Amour,* Mme de Villedieu attempts to establish more noble reasons for it. Thus she indicates that Bellegarde was one of the Dauphin's pages at a time when he was actually lieutenant in his uncle's battalion (Mézeray, II, 719). In this way, the suggestion is made that the duc de Savoie and Bellegarde would have naturally been allies.

Other minor points of "divergence" in the nouvelle serve principally to accentuate some aspect of Bellegarde's character or personality. He did not inherit the title of marquis, for example, because his uncle did not possess it; and, furthermore, the Maréchal de Termes willed his title and arms to Bellegarde's younger brother, Jean de Saint-Lary. By according him both the title of marquis and the rank of maréchal (which he did acquire), Mme de Villedieu renders all of his subsequent attitudes and actions that much more reprehensible since Bellegarde proves himself to be unworthy of both.[24]

Nouvelles III and IV:

("The Prince Challenges Passions's Reign")[25]

The last story in *Les Désordres de
l'Amour* is clearly the most "historical" in the
sense that the text of the third and fourth
nouvelles constitutes in places summaries and
finally veritable textual repetitions of the
historical document. Its hero, Anne d' Anglure,
baron de Givry, is found not only in Mézeray but
in other historical accounts as well.[26] So when
Mme de Villedieu writes that "il avoit une connoissance parfaite des belles lettres et des
mathématiques; il possédoit les langues grecque,
latine, & toutes les langues vivantes de l'Europe
. . .et des charmes qui lui gagnoient tous les
coeurs" (pp. 120-122), there is nothing inherently
romanesque in this description. Rather, the
portrait appears extremely historical since
Mézeray himself writes:

> Sa grande connaissance des belles-lettres,
> des langues et des mathématiques, animée par
> un beau feu et par une brillante vivacité
> d'esprit rendoit son entretien si agréable
> qu'il passoit pour l'un des plus braves et
> des plus vaillants de la cour. (III, 1088)

Although Mme de Villedieu does not contradict her source when she suggests that Givry was
an intimate member of the Guise household, this
precision can not be found in Mézeray. Yet, this
very fact is at least suggested in another
seventeenth-century document to which Mme de
Villedieu probably had access: the works of
Brantôme.[27]

The hero was, as indeed the nouvelle states,
"à la tête de la cavalerie légère de France"; and
he was "gouverneur" of Brie (Mézeray, III, 242).
Moreover, Mme de Villedieu's text accords Givry
precisely the active military role that the

historical document suggests. He participated, for example, in each of the military campaigns that *Les Désordres de l'Amour* describes: the disengagement of the Loire river (Mézeray, III, 640-644); his actions at the bridge of Samois (III, 786); the sieges of Paris and of Rouen (III, 829, 912), etc. Similarly, the novelist adheres closely to the facts in her allusion to the dilemma caused by Henri de Navarre's ascension to the throne (Mézeray, III, 688-798). She also accurately describes Givry's acceptance of the new king and his role in the stabilization of this rule.

Surely, one would speculate, Mme de Villedieu resorts to a pure *romanesque* invention when she "creates" a truce that allows the hero to enter Paris for the first time to converse with the princesse de Guise. Yet, though no cease-fire is mentioned in Mézeray, the historian does in fact state that negotiations were in progress.

Even the episode of Givry's action at the bridge of Samois--the shipment of wheat to Paris-- comes directly from history.[28] Whereas Mme de Villedieu mentions that it was a question of "six mille muids de bled," Mézeray specifies three thousand. And although in *Histoire de France* the motives for the gesture appear at first to be purely monetary gain, the historian does suggest more *"galant"* reasons for it later in his *Abrégé:*

> Les Parisiens n'avoient presqu'autre provision que trois mille muids de bled et dix mille muids de vin que Givry laissa passer au pont de Chamoy [sic], pour un présent qu'on lui fit de 10.000 écus, et par une secrete complaisance pour Mademoiselle de Guise, dont il 'étoit fort piqué.[29]

Although this, apparently, did not constitute an unprecedented gesture on Givry's part and although he was hardly the sole officer to allow the blockades to be penetrated during sieges, Mézeray gives the same importance to this particular incident as does Mme de Villedieu. For whereas on other occasions and for other officers it was usually a question of small gifts ("des vivres et des rafraichissements à leurs amis. . .et particulièrement aux dames"--Mézeray, III, 521), this particular gesture seems indeed to have constituted a dangerous indiscretion, as Mézeray writes, "ce fut presque la seule provision de vivres qui entra dans Paris et sans laquelle la faim l'eut étranglé dedans peu de semaines" (III, 786).

And finally, the hero's death letter to Mlle de Guise strikes the modern reader as unquestionably too *romanesque* to contain any historical verity. Yet this letter exists integrally as part of a manuscript in the Arsenal library of Paris.[30]

The other two principal protagonists in this last story, Mlle de Guise and Bellegarde, are likewise historical personages. This latter, Roger de Saint-Lary de Bellegarde (1563-1646) appears to have ingratiated himself with Henri IV for whom he functioned as "maître de sa garde-robe," "premier gentilhomme de sa chambre," and "Grand Ecuyer" (Mézeray, III, 513). He was not, however, a marquis as the nouvelle indicates, though his descendants did acquire this title. Most assuredly, Bellegarde and Givry knew each other since they were both important military officers; nevertheless, the intimate friendship accorded them by Mme de Villedieu is historically untenable. In the context of the plot, this invention serves to accentuate the tragedy of the situation.

As for Mlle de Guise, the seventeenth-century perhaps knew her best as Milagarde, a character from l'*Alcandre*.[31] This anonymous work, which in 1675 was already in its sixteenth edition, was thought to have been written by the princesse de Guise. This princess, Louise Marguerite de Lorraine (1577-1631), was the daughter of Henri, duc de Guise and Catherine de Clèves. She is described by Mézeray as "fraichement élevée, très belle et très honnête . . ." (III, 1091).

As in the previous two stories, even the minor characters are historical: the baron de Vins (a member of the League party; and though not a baron, he is mentioned in Mézeray as president of the *parlement* of Aix--III, 719, 732, 802); Mme de Guise (Catherine de Clèves, comtesse d'Eu, married to Henri de Lorraine); Mme de Nemours (Anne d'Este, widow of François de Guise, and mother of the duc de Guise assassinated in 1588); the duc de Maine (Mayenne), etc.

In fact, Mme de Maugiron alone appears to be an invented character--not only in this particular nouvelle but in Mme de Villedieu's text as a whole. Mézeray's *Histoire* does include a Laurent de Maugiron who was, as the nouvelle indicates, Lieutenant-Général in the governments of Dauphiné and of Bourgogne. He was married to a relative, Jeanne de Maugiron, but neither Mézeray nor any other historian mentions a second marriage, though it is entirely possible.

This "second" Mme de Maugiron, nevertheless, receives a historical legitimacy and specificity as she appears in the nouvelle as part of the entourage of Queen Louise. Consequently, her itinerary is "real" because the novelist has this heroine at precisely those places where *Histoire de France* informs us the queen was residing at any particular time. When one reads in the nouvelle, for instance, that in the spring of 1588 Mme de Maugiron "étoit demeurée à Chinon auprés de la Reine Louise d'où elle lui [à Givry] écrivoit par tous les courriers," the detail emerges directly from Mézeray who writes that "Ayant donc fait conduire la Reine à Chinon afin qu'elle fut éloignée des dangers, [le Roi] commença dès les premiers jours de juin à marcher à la tête de son armée" (III, 644).

Besides the invention of Mme de Maugiron, the nouvelle offers as few minor disparities in relation to the historical documents: for example, Givry, just prior to his death, was not one of the king's negotiators with the duc de Mayenne and the duc de Guise (p. 199); Mme de Villedieu adds this detail apparently to explain the hero's frequent contact with the Guises.

In spite of this, this final story, as was noted earlier and as the copious notes by Cuénin in her introduction to Mme de Villedieu's text suggest, is composed often of sentences or paragraphs that summarize longer passages in

Mézeray's text. For this reason, Mme de Villedieu remains extremely accurate in her account of the activities and logistics of Henri IV and his forces during the years in question as when, to give but one example, she describes the king's personal involvement in the siege of Rouen (p. 167). And as the following example--again to cite but one--will illustrate, Mme de Villedieu from time to time quite literally *embeds* the historical *énoncé* into her own text. In her description of the important siege of Rouen (December, 1590) where Givry is gravely wounded, Mme de Villedieu writes:

> Les assiegez faisoient des sorties
> furieuses & presque tous les jours il
> se faisoit des escarmouches, qu'on
> pouvoit appeller de sanglans combats.
> Givry fut dangereusement blessé à
> l'épaule dans une de ces rencontres,
> & la tristesse dont il étoit possedé
> augmentant le peril où le mettoit sa
> blessure, les chirurgiens le jugerent
> a l'extremité de sa vie. Le Roi
> aimoit tendrement ce jeune homme, &
> doutoit qu'il y eût personne de son
> armée capable de remplir la place
> qu'il occupoit. Il déclara si haute-
> ment ce doute qu'il fit plusieurs
> mécontens; il en méprisa même les
> murmures. (pp. 167-178)

The entire paragraph seems to border on plagiarism when one reads the following passage in Mézeray's text:

> Furieuse sortie des assiégés le 26
> Fevrier. . .Tous les jours de
> sanglants combats dont le plus
> mémorable fut celui qui se fit dans
> l'abbaye de Grammont au-dessus du
> faux bourg Saint-Sever où Givry,
> colonel de la cavalerie légère fut si
> grièvement blessé à l'épaule que le
> Roi en desespera de sa vie. Il en
> réchappa néanmoins contre l'attente

de tout de monde. Mais le Roi, pour
en avoir trop témoigné de regret,
perdit François Juvenal des Ursins de
la Chapelle, d'autant qu'ayant dit
que si Givry mouroit il n'y avoit
personne qu'il pût substituer en sa
place. La Chapelle s'imagina que par
ces paroles il le déclaroit indigne
de cette charge laquelle il lui avoit
fait esperer, et le ressentiment
qu'il en eut fut si violent qu'il se
jeta peu après dans le parti de la
Ligue. (III, 942)

It is significant that this last story is
also the one where the king *re-appears*. The weak,
ineffective and passive Henri III of the first two
stories (he has abdicated his authority to passion
in the first and is totally absent in the second)
is assassinated and reincarnated here as the
active and dynamic Henri IV. This, then, is the
only one of the three stories where the monarch
appears as a *speaking* character.[32] Moreover, he
is presented as a valiant military leader and as
an aggressive yet sensitive domestic conciliator--
oftentimes the voice of wisdom and reason in
direct opposition to the rages and follies of
passion.[33] He emerges as the stabilizing force
(*ordre*) in the confusion of political and personal
disorders: ". . .le Roi, . . .qui sçavoit par-
faitement les affaires de Givry, l'envoya
chercher, & se servit si à propos du pouvoir qu'il
avoit sur son esprit, qu'il en calma le *désordre*"
(p. 189, emphasis added).

Yet, in spite of the fact that the mere presence of the king commands order ("le Roi fut à
peine entré dans Paris que le calme s'y rétablit
comme si jamais il n'y avoit eu de *désordre*"--p.
198), passion proves to be an unheeding and sedi-
tious subject. This becomes even more apparent in
the princesse de Guise's insensitivity and irre-
verence towards Henri IV's personal interventions
and touching supplications on Givry's behalf:
"Elle ne fit que sourire des reproches du
Roi. . ." (p. 207). She is passion personified.

If one can delineate the first story in

36

terms of a general movement from the power of the king to the power of the mistress, i.e., from politics to passion, and if one can speak of the second as the complete "parenthesization" of the political to the profit of passion, then one can characterize this final story as the attempt to integrate the political and the passional. This proves to be, however, an impossible coexistence as passion, this illegitimate and merciless tyrant, invariably asserts itself as a challenge to the legitimate prince.

** ** **

In summary, it would seem from the preceding observations that even when she deviates from her historical source, Mme de Villedieu strives and succeeds in doing so within the bounds of a historical truth and *vraisemblance*. Again, as a result, not only are the historical context and atmosphere of the period maintained, but the psychology and personality of the principal per-sonages are likewise very closely respected and followed.

The queen mother appears in the first nouvelle of *Les Désordres de l'Amour* exactly as she appears in *Histoire de France*: shrewd and manipulative. Therefore, when Mme de Villedieu, as novelist, needs to evoke the character of this queen, she remains within the confines of a historical truth and verisimilitude by having Catherine mastermind, for example, certain sche-mes. Mme de Sauve is as beautiful and as repre-hensible in "fact" as she is in fiction. Mme de Villedieu, as I shall have occasion to examine more closely in a forthcoming chapter, merely lends her words and actions that highlight these qualities. The same is true, in the first nouvelle, for the minor characters: Henri de Navarre, though somewhat of a flirt, is an admirable nobleman; Du Guast is ambitious and un-scrupulous; Henri III is weak and easily mani-pulated; and if he is not as piteous in fiction as he appears in the document, it is undoubtedly because his role in the nouvelle has been reduced to that of a peripheral character.

As a careful examination reveals, the novelist, in her second nouvelle, again respects the
characters' personalities and psychology by representing them just as history suggests that they
were: the Maréchal de Bellegarde was indeed,
according to Mézeray, a disgraced man. Mme de
Villedieu merely fills in the gaps of the official
document by showing how his passions influenced
his behavior. It is reasonable to expect that an
ambitious military officer, should he become
disgraced politically, would fault especially a
marriage that had been a political liability; and
he would undoubtedly no longer have any use for
such a wife. This fictitious utterance in the
mouth of Bellegarde makes him a villain in the
eyes of the reader. Yet this is consistent with
the impression that one gets from Mézeray who, as
historian, leaves the reader to conclude that the
Maréchal's military maneuvers and political sche-
mes constituted abhorrent acts. As for Mme de
Bellegarde, it is very plausible that a hurt and
dejected wife would be tempted to seek revenge
against her husband, as Mme de Villedieu suggests.

In the third and fourth nouvelles, the
characters are once more the mirror images of the
ones found in history. Mme de Villedieu follows
the sources in portraying Henri IV as admirable
and kind and in depicting Bellegarde as somewhat
mystified and less than scrupulous. In the
nouvelle, as in history, Mlle de Guise is ego-
tistical and capricious, just as Givry himself
appears to be the perfect nobleman and lover.
Indeed, none of the protagonists in *Les Désordres
de l'Amour* are presented as idealized "personnages
de romans." They rarely display a *grandeur*; they
are "real."

Even when the literary text more or less
fictionalizes, i.e., speculates, about the behavior of one of the characters, it is within the
bounds both of human psychology and historical
fact as they were understood by its author. Here,
history (under the guise of literature) conforms
to the "realities" of human nature; but equally,
human psychology (in literature) conforms to
history's "truth."

Rarely indeed does Mme de Villedieu actually,

that is to say, deliberately and *seriously,* modify the historical account as she read and understood it. She does change a few details or omit a few others; but, on the whole, none of the modifications or omissions of historical data seriously compromise "les vérités importantes de l'histoire générale." Mme de Villedieu, after having read history, sets out to deconstruct it or to select details from the documents and to add a few speculations of her own that allow her to re-construct or to *extend* the historical narrative. As a result of this deconstruction and subsequent reconstruction, her own narrative "flows," obeying certain laws and principles concerning human motivation and psychology. The writer of literature, in effect, has isolated those elements from the annals that confirm the latent "lessons" of history. For, if the nouvelle is to compose an *exemplum,* as she wished it to, then it must adhere to one overriding rule: "*Solum quod facit ad rem est narradum*"[34] --where *rem* (or *res*) is the moral truth of the poetic maxims.

Evidently, this selection process or this veritable *découpage* of the historical source is hardly a disinterested or undiscriminating activity. History, most assuredly, does not enter into the nouvelle completely unchanged--that is to say, the nouvelle is not, nor can it be, an exact copy of the historical document. One immediate result of this deconstruction of the historical source is that there are "traces" of it within the literary text. It is in order to explore further and to explicate the consequences of and the types of assumptions made by this kind of literary activity that I shall turn my attention now to an examination of the modes of representation of the historical materials in *Les Désordres de l'Amour:* the process of *énonciation,* the literary event.

NOTES

CHAPTER ONE

1. François Eudes de Mézeray, *Histoire de France contenant le règne du Roi Henri III et celui du Roi Henri IV jusqu'à la Paix de Vervins inclusivement*, 3 Vol. (Paris: Mathieu Guillemot, 1651). For my remarks in this preliminary chapter, I am heavily indebted to the introduction and notes to the Cuénin edition of the text. After having read the historical account in Mézeray, I find Cuénin's observations to be perceptive and accurate. In some ways, what I propose here represents a synthesis and an expansion of her suggestions.

2. These are, of course, kinds of questions that critics have formulated and have attempted to answer for some time. In 1862, for example, Alexis Chassang published one of the earliest studies on the topic with his *Histoire du roman et de ses rapports avec l'histoire dans l'antiquité grecque et latine* (Paris: Didier). It is my contention that these questions can be re-formulated and further elucidated in light of Mme de Villedieu's specific case.

3. Possible sources for Mme de Villedieu: Brantôme, *Vies des Hommes Illustres et Grands Capitaines Français* (1665), and his *Vies des Dames Illustres* (1666); P. Anselme, *Histoire de la Maison Royale en France et de Grands Officiers de la Couronne* (1674); D'Aubigné, *Histoire Universelle* (1616); E. Davila, *Histoire des Guerres Civiles* (1642); Chiverni, *Mémoires d'Etat* (1636).

4. Generally, for both the novel and history in the seventeenth century "facts" were not sacred; the historian (and this dates back perhaps to his Greek and Latin predecessors who, above all else, were moralists) had not yet clearly defined the limits of his science/art. History was to please and was to be limited to the "beaux sujets" and was to be used ultimately to instruct princes and

their ministers. (See, for example, P. Anselme, *Histoire Généalogique,* Loyson, 1674, and note 5 below).

5. It is Barbara R. Woshinsky (*La Princesse de Clèves: The Tension of Elegance* [Paris: Mouton, 1973]) who best summarizes the "psychological connection" between history and fiction of the period:

> In the psychological realm, seventeenth century history and fiction already were quite close together: they both strongly emphasized the role of the passions in human life. Since historians attributed historical change to the actions of great men, history, like fiction, had to explore personal motives and feelings. St-Réal, who was both a novelist and historian, defined history's province thus: "Savoir l'histoire, c'est connaître les hommes qui en fournissent la matière, c'est juger de ces hommes sainement; étudier l'histoire, c'est étudier les motifs, les opinions et les passions des hommes, pour en connaître tous les ressorts, tous les tours et les détours. . . (*De l'Usage de l'histoire*, 2nd ed. [Paris, 1672], 3)

> Seventeen century thinkers and historians inherited this view of the passions from the Renaissance. The Renaissance historians, drawing on both classical and Christian traditions, saw man as a creature who was both dominated by his passions and (who) used them to dominate others. Machiavelli (*The Prince*) explained the politics of Florence by reference to the jealousy, zeal, ambition or pride of its leaders. Their passions spurred them on to glorious achievements, but their control over them was imperfect: the same passions that caused leaders to rise also brought about their precipitate fall. (48-49)

Thinkers during Descartes' time also assumed that passions motivated all human activity--good and evil. For Descartes (*Traité des Passions*), however, man was capable of mastering his passions to lead a "moral" life. After Descartes, other Classical thinkers (La Rochefoucauld, for example) continued to consider passions to be the basis of human activity but they stressed man's inability to control them at all times.

Because the historian would be interested in the human and personal causes of history, he might be tempted "to abandon facts for psychological conjecture and even pure invention, 'à interpréter des actes qu'il connaît mal, à reconstituer, au gré de sa fantaisie, les antécédents moraux d'événements dont les sources authentiques ne donnent qu'un brut exposé. Et très vite l'on en arrive ainsi au roman'" (G. Dulong, *l'Abbé de Saint-Réal, Etude sur les rapports de l'histoire et du Roman au XVIIe Siècle* (Paris, 1921), 1, p. 41)--Woshinsky, p.50.

6. History and fiction were related for esthetic reasons too: i.e., mode of representation. "En effet l'Histoire nous représente les choses avenues et véritables, du même air à peu près que la poésie nous dépeint les posibles et les vraisemblables" (La Mothe le Vayer, *Discours de l'histoire*, in *Oeuvres*, IV, p. 300). In fact, both history and fiction were subject to the Classical demands for *vraisemblance* and *bienséance* (see, e.g., Woshinsky, Chapter III).

7. Mézeray vol. III, pp. 32-100 as compared to Mme de Villedieu's account. These events will be examined more closely later in this chapter.

8. Marguerite de Saluces is mentioned also by Brantôme in his *Vies des Dames Illustres.*

9. After what appears to be a brief introduction, this first nouvelle is divided into three sections separated by three aphoristic poems--the significance of which will be explored in the second part of this study. But since the nouvelles are relatively unknown stories, a somewhat detailed résumé of the plot of this first nouvelle is provided to facilitate the reader's familiarity with its structure. This, in turn, will ultimately give full weight to my present observations. Consult

10. I should perhaps clarify my use of the terms "history" and "historical." When I speak of Mme de Villedieu's texts as adhering to historical fact or "truth," I mean this in a seventeen-century perspective, i.e., what the novelist herself read and accepted as historical fact. For the modern reader, it can perhaps be easily contested that much of what Mme de Villedieu writes (and what I myself label as "historical") is in fact inaccurate insofar as it is based on the fallacies found in Mézeray. (For a discussion of Mézeray's historical method, see Wilfred H. Evans, *Mézeray, l'Historien et la Conception de l'Histoire Au XVIIe Siècle* (Paris: Gamber, 1930.) Yet, I am not concerned here with the historicity of *Les Désordres de l'Amour* from a modern perspective; "history" for me *is* Mézeray.

11. Mézeray, Vol. III, pp. 1-32. Henceforth, all references to Mézeray will be included in the text in parentheses and will indicate the volume and page.

12. All page notations refer to the Cuénin edition of *Les Désordres de l'Amour* and will be included in the text in parentheses. In matters of spelling and punctuation, I shall respect this edition (which is based on the 1702 copy of the nouvelles found in a collection of the author's work). For example, acute accents are omitted but are sometimes used to denote a more closed sound than in modern French (e.g. aprés); circumflexes are widely used, sometimes seemingly for no reason; the ending "ez" is used for "és" and "ès," and other particularities.

13. For example, Mme de Villedieu describes the confrontation between Monsieur and the King of Navarre (p. 32) as taking place in the "jardin des Thuilleries" whereas Mézeray describes it as taking place when the court was still at Lyon: "Il se rencontra en concurrence et par conséquent en pique avec Monsieur, premièrement pour une autre dame et encore à deux mois de la pour la même de Sauve" (III, 44)--cited by Cuénin, p. 32.

14. For example, she describes Dugua, a minor

character, as having a love affair with a certain woman (p. 46) for which no basis can be found in her sources; but this hardly affects the "reading" of the historical document.

15. This source is Marguerite de Valois' *Mémoires* which Mme de Villedieu certainly read and to which she may be referring when she writes in her first nouvelle: ". . .comme les Mémoires sur lesquels je fais ce commentaire en font foi (la guerre) eut sa source dans les intrigues d'amour que je viens d'écrire" (p. 65).

16. See the Introduction to the Cuénin edition of *Les Désordres de l'Amour*, xxxvi.

17. As will be seen in Part Two of this study, this second nouvelle is divided into two "parts" by two intervening poems. Again, as this may be an unfamiliar story, a complete account of it is provided to facilitate the comprehension of my remarks. See Appendix B.

18. That is to say, the *historical document* as it would have been defined during the Classical period. French (national) history seems to have been a stylized genre of an almost rigid structure of events: the genealogies of French kings. (See Michel Tyvaert, "L'image du Roi. . .au XVIIe Siècle," *Revue d'Histoire Modèrne et Contemporaine*, 26 (1974), 523-547.)

19 The way that the intercepted letter constitutes such an important aspect for the progression of the narrative is expounded upon in the course of my analysis of the function of the poetic maxim (pp. 53-74).

20. These seemingly "invented" scenes, which are also analyzed in Part Two of this study, are perhaps what truly distinguish the nouvelles from the historical document.

21. "Tous les documents de l'époque attestent en effet que le Maréchal légua tous ses biens à son petit neveu Roger de Saint-Lary, seigneur de Bellegarde. Ils étaient d'ailleurs fort minces . . .La condition indiquée ensuite (par Mme de Villedieu) est purement imaginaire mais elle

s'inspire d'une vieille tradition de la noblesse que les lecteurs connaissent bien" (Cuénin, p. 78, note 18).

There is equally no record of any heir contesting Termes' will (consult Appendix B) as he had only two nephews (Roger and his younger brother, Jean de Saint-Lary) and both were included equally in the will. This second addition constitutes a logical extension of the first (the stipulation of the will) and neither seriously affects the reading of history as found in Mézeray.

22. Du Guast is not listed, for instance, as accompanying the duc d'Anjou to Poland as Mme de Villedieu recounts (p. 88); the duc de Modene (Modenne) was not a part of the duc de Savoie's plans for peace, etc.

23. As a comparison between the nouvelle and *Histoire de France* reveals and as Cuénin indicates, Bellegarde's alleged confrontation with the queen mother (pp. 99-101), for example, occurs in the nouvelle at the time when he was, in all likelihood, in Lyon as he had just been made Maréchal; the queen mother does not send Dugua to restore her favor with the king (p. 94), he goes on his own behalf; but it would be somewhat of a digression to include Dugua's personal motivation (Mézeray, III, 29).

24. In this same vein, the nouvelle fails to mention (as indeed history suggest) that it was both Bellegarde and the duc de Savoie who propose Damville's reconciliation with the king. By excluding Bellegarde from this endeavor, the novelist does not present him as blindly ambitious until after the persecutions of his new bride. The nouvelle thereby suggests that it was this persecution that rendered the baron progressively corrupt. This is not a totally accurate portrait, for although his connubial situation may have influenced his political and military efforts, Bellegarde's ambitious undertakings unquestionably predate his marriage to Marguerite.

25. The third and fourth nouvelles--which for the purposes of my comments here one could subtitle as the "Prince Challenges Passion's Reign"--

constitute a single story. For a précis of the
story, consult Appendix C.

26.   Chiverni (Philippe Hurault, comte de),
Mémoires d'Etat (Paris: Billaine, 1636), describes him as a gentlemen endowed with so many good
and rare qualities that few men in all of France
could be compared to him (p. 169).   Davila
(*Histoire des Guerres Civiles*, 2 vol., 1642)
praises "la douceur de ses moeurs et l'accortise
de son esprit où se trouvait jointe encore la con-
naissance des bonnes lettres, qualités illustres
qui lui gagnaient les volontés d'un chacun, le
faisaient aimer et même louer de ses propres
ennemies" (Vol. II, p. 441)--cited by Cuénin, p.
120.

27.   Brantôme, *Oeuvres Complètes* (Paris: la
Société d'Histoire de France, 1864), Vol. VI, p.
169.

28.   "Le Pont de Samois bridoit le haut de la
Seine.   Givry, qui commandoit dans cette place
avoit accoutumé, avant la bataille d'Ivry, d'en
laisser passer pour de l'argent.   Il fit lors dif-
ficulté de leur continuer le même marché; en
effet, le service du Roi ne lui devoit pas per-
mettre de le tenir.   Mais il ne leur serroit le
passage que pour les obliger à ouvrir davantage
leur bourse, si bien que lorsqu'ils l'eurent
assuré de 100.000 écus, il laissa couler près de
3.000 muids de grains, et plus de 10.000 muids de
vin" Mézeray, III, 786)--quoted by Cuénin, p. 143.

29. *Abrégé Chronologique ou Extrait de l'Histoire
de France*, Vol. II, p. 1226--cited by Cuénin, p.
144.

30.   "Lettre de Monsieur de Givry à Mademoiselle
de Lorraine, qui a esté depuis Mme la Princesse de
Conty, en allant combattre au siège de Laon",
Conrat, *Manuscrits*, ref. 4.110, Vol. V, p. 1--
quoted by Cuénin, p. 206.

31.   *Histoire des Amours du Grand Alcandre*
appeared in 1629 and is thought now to have been
written by a certain Mme de Simier.   For a comparison of this work with Mme de Villedieu's
texts, see Bruce Morrissette (*The Life and Works*

of Catherine Desjardins).

32.   As will be seen during my discussion of the
modes of representation in Mme de Villedieu's
texts, whether a character "speaks" or not becomes
a critical issue in the narrative scheme.

33.   As will be seen in my chapter on the explicit
shifter, the king re-emerges in this last story
quite literally as an enunciator of moral maxims
and as a guarantor of political order. It is precisely because his subjects ignore his *orders* that
conflict and chaos arise: "alors les deux rivaux,
oubliant les ordres du Roi, se lancerent l'un sur
l'autre avec une fureur sans égale" (p. 197).

34.   "Only that which is about the *subject* is to
be narrated."   (Karlheinz Stierle, "l'Histoire
comme   Example,   l'Exemple   comme   Histoire,"
Poétique, 16 (1972), 176-198.)   And the subject
for Mme de Villedieu is *love*.   Her reading of
history is a conscious or unconscious filtering.
She sees as *significant* (i.e., historical) only
those events and episodes that confirm certain
universal maxims on human nature.

PART II
THE LITERARY EVENT
(ÉNONCIATION)

My reading of *Les Désordres de l'Amour* in the preceding chapter has demonstrated that Mme de Villedieu exploits a well-known seventeenth-century document for the development and structuration of her plots. This exploitation or this embedment of the historical *énoncé* into the nouvelle renders it a particularly interesting text because it allows the reader, in the final analysis, to reconstruct the process by which the nouvelle traces and theorizes about its own production.

As was suggested earlier in this study (Introduction), this text modulates periodically, and at times almost imperceptibly, between two modes: the narrative and the discursive. It is characterized by a shift from *récit historique* to discours.[1] It will be by examining this passage--one that might be characterized as a modulation from history (the *énoncé*) to literature (the *énonciation*)--that one will be able to comprehend the circumstances under which this transformation takes place and the consequences of the coexistence of these two instances: the temporality of the event itself and the temporality of the evocation of the event. By identifying these points or "instances" of passage by means of an examination of the form and the degree of the representation, one will come to terms with the subject of the *énonciation*: how and where the enunciator (*énonciateur*-- the act and the agent) is implicated in the *énoncé*. Generally speaking, one can identify two kinds of "shifters" in Mme de Villedieu's text that can be tentatively labeled as commentarial or *exegetic* and organizatory or *logistic*.[2]

The exegetic shifter assumes several forms and includes, first, all those parts of the text where the narrator intervenes in his own name to judge or comment on the events and characters. This is usually characterized by the first-person pronoun and the utilization of certain tenses such as the present, the future, and the perfect. These tenses, as Emile Benveniste shows, assume invariably the presence of a narrating agent in a temporal sequence. Whereas the aorist (*passé simple*), for example, could be labeled "static" in the sense that its use indicates no relationship to the time of the one who uses it, the perfect (*passé composé*), on the other hand, introduces a link between the past event and the present instance where it is recalled. It indicates the time of the speaker and constitutes thus the tense that must be employed if one wishes to represent an event and to tie it to the present moment of discourse.[3]

The exegetic shifter includes, secondly, fragments of the text where, on the contrary, the narrator pretends to withdraw completely form it to let the events "tell themselves." This is frequently in the form of scenes and "objective" passages where there is a total absence of any sign of the narrator.[4]

The logistic shifter, in form similar to the exegetic, consists of all the signs whereby the narator arranges and organizes his own discourse (comments) in referring explicitly to it as such. This second kind of shifter is characterized by meta-narrative stances within the text that indicate the direction of a *discours* in relation to the form of the text.

On a very obvious level, but by no means the only one, the penetration of the *discours* into the *récit historique* can be found in the form of *Les Désordres de l'Amour*: a mixed genre of poetry, in the form of maxims, and prose. As perhaps both a commentarial and an organizatory shifter, the maxims in verse deserve careful consideration. As a shifter of exegeses, they generally contain the "meaning" that the narrator explicitly assigns to the events of history; as a shifter of logistics, they operate to announce, to recall, to accentuate, and to direct the progressive development of a particular discourse on history, the *discours*.

Yet, in addition to this obvious shifter constituted by the poetic maxim (or as I shall label them, the un-integrated maxims), the text also contains inconspicuous maxims in prose that are totally and sometimes almost imperceptibly integrated into the *récit historique*, the diegesis itself. It is towards this un-integrated maxim, however, that I shall direct my attention in the

first chapter of this section, reserving a second
chapter for a closer examination of this second
kind of maxim and shifter.

CHAPTER TWO

THE MAXIM AS "EXTRA-TEXTUAL"

If, as I shall attempt to postulate, one of the obvious ways that Mme de Villedieu transforms, so to speak, a historical document into a nouvelle is by creating the explicit "presence" and "present" (tense) of a narrator--that is to say, by creating a conscience that appears "between" the lines of official history--then a logical place to begin an examination of this transformation is with the poetic maxims in the nouvelles. The narrative act and agent are never more evident than here. These maxims are predominately in the present as opposed to the past tense (aorist) of the nouvelle as a whole. And although it may be argued that this atemporal present of universal and eternal truths may not necessarily correspond to the present tense of the narrator at the moment of *énonciation*, it must invariably be a sign, an effect, a trace of his presence in the text.

First of all, these maxims are not arbitrarily *arranged* within the text. They are not integrated textually within the nouvelle but are numbered and set apart both spatially and formally. I mean by this of course that it is a question of two different literary genres or forms. Indeed, one of the more conspicuous characteristics of this text by Mme de Villedieu is its dualistic and fragmented nature: the body of what is essentially a prose narrative is pierced by intervening verses that fragment it into several parts of varying lengths.

And secondly, the maxims are not necessarily *drawn from* history--thus symbolically in the nouvelles they *precede* the prose segments into which the text is divided--but rather the historical materials seem to be selected to illustrate the truth of the maxims. It appears as if it is the aphorism that legitimizes the historical events and not the reverse. The question is immediately raised, of course, as to the force behind this selection and arrangement.

The seventeenth-century public was accustomed to and undoubtedly found esthetically pleasing works that combine prose and verse; and, in this respect, *Les Désordres de l'Amour*, like some of the other works by Mme de Villedieu, can be inscribed in the mode *précieux*.[5] Elsewhere in her works, however, the poetry seems to have been more or less gratuitous. In these nouvelles, by contrast, the verse is in the form of moral maxims that have both a *syntactic* and a *semantic* function. Syntactically, they obviously punctuate the story at regular intervals; but how are they incorporated into the nouvelles semantically?

Simply stated, one can say that these aphoristic poems contain the essential elements of the nouvelles in microscopic form; and, at the same time, they serve as commentary on the plot. In other words, the relationship between the verse and the segments of prose to which it corresponds is a metaphorical one: the aphorisms consist of the elements of the plot (prose) *reduced* to its "lowest common denominator." Thus, inversely, the plot in its totality is the syntagmatization of these narrative atoms or mini-plots; and, therefore, as the narrative expansion of the verse, the prose constitutes the *exemplum* of the maxim's basic truth.

The first nouvelle in *Les Désordres de l'Amour* is divided into three parts punctuated by three poems. But preceding the first poem and the initial prose segment is a kind of prologue which itself displays the following subtitle or statment in italics and set apart from the body of the text: " *Que l'Amour est le ressort de toutes les autres passions de l'âme.*" In reconstructing the essentials of the plot of this first nouvelle, not only can one expose how the entire story is the verification of this prefacing sentence, but one can also explore in detail the relationship between the three maxims and the prose into which they are embedded in order to identify the literary "activity" of this novelist.

This introductory maxim exposes, as this chapter will venture to demonstrate, the essence of the nouvelle, verse *and* prose, compressed into an apothegm. It is its moral, its lesson. In placing this sentence in this initial position, Mme de Villedieu accomplishes two things that deserve additional comment: at the outset she provides the plan, the "roadmap" with which her text is to be read; and, in so doing, she positions a "voice" between the text (the events of history) and its recipient. Secondly, (and this is a direct consequence of the first), by channelling the reader's attention to certain aspects of the nouvelle, she prejudices him in effect by legislating and adjudicating "how" the story is to be perceived; and in doing this she denies the recipient of the narrative any *liberté de lecteur*. The result is that of a closed text. Its lesson is not absorbed in it for the reader to extract but is presented in its concentrated form. Thus, in prescribing its own "meaning," the text attempts to preclude any insight that the reader might possibly supply because its structure fails to provide any "gaps" or lacuna which he might possibly fill.

In this opening *sententia* ("Que l'Amour est le ressort de toutes les autres passions de l'âme") one key word is *ressort* (i.e., *énergie, moteur*); for just as love will constitute the *force motrice* that will govern the entire spectrum of human activity and sentiment in the history that is about to unfold, so too is this *sententia* the force, the energy, or to borrow a term from linguistics, the "grammar" from which the story's manifold articulations will germinate.

This prologue establishes the historical context of the action which opens with the ascension of Henri III to the French throne. The prevailing tone here is optimistic and somewhat *romanesque*, suggesting perhaps that one is about to be submerged into one of the numerous heroic narratives that populated and at a certain point even dominated the seventeenth-century literary scene.[6] Henri would certainly appear to be the *romanesque* hero *par excellence*: in addition to his physical "comeliness," it is recalled that he was a gallant and brave prince, having won two decisive military victories before the age of eighteen. He thus seemed destined for a long, glorious reign and all of France was pregnant with hope that his coronation would signal the beginning of a pleasant, peaceful, and productive period in her history.

"The Sign as Dissimulation"

In terms of the narrative configuration (i.e., on the one hand, the relationships between the characters themselves, and, on the other, the relationship between the narrator/reader and the characters) the problem posed ultimately in this first nouvelle is that of the sign.[7] Metaphorically, one can speak of it in terms of the problem of the relationship between the signifier and the signified: the sign in its verticality, found here in the form of a dislocation between the characters' actions and their intentions, their words and their sentiments. This is to say that the reader, just as if he were a character within the story, must constantly be aware of the degree to which the historical characters' actions and words (signifiers) correspond to their intentions and sentiments (signified). In examining the themes and the thematics of this first nouvell, one

will in effect be tracing the process of the
demystification of the sign, of the characters'
outward appearances.

The first part of the nouvelle begins with
Maxime I:

Mais l'Amour, ce tiran des plus illustres âmes,
Cet ennemi secret de nos prosperitez,
Qui, sous de faux plaisirs, nous déguisant ses
  flames,
Nous fait passer des maux pour des félicitez;
Aux yeux du Nouveau Roi fait briller ses chimeres.
Il se laissa charmer à leur vaine douceur,
Et leur voluptez mensongeres,
En seduisant les sens, amolissent le coeur.

This first maxim illustrates precisely how
the reader is going to be guided and tutored in
his reading of history. The heroic and optimistic
(one could say almost Cornelian) atmosphere that
characterizes the prologue (and which perhaps has
already been somewhat tinted by the opening
proverb) is immediately and irrevocably put into
question with the adversative "Mais" that begins
the poem. The reader is hereby warned not to be
duped; for Love, this tyrant of even the most
illustrious souls, is in fact a *hidden* enemy of
man's happiness that, under *false* pleasures, *dis-*
guises its ravages to make one's afflictions
appear as blessings. Indeed, the theme of dissimulation, false pretenses, deceptions, etc. is one
that dominates the entire nouvelle. As the reader
will see, confusion and disorder are conceived and
propagated because of a breakdown in communication; the historical personages do not say what
they mean; they are not what they appear to be.

This maxim suggests that Love will not only
constitute a character in this story but that it
will be the most important personage ("ce tiran").
One is struck by the rapid succession of terms
that serve to contrast and contradict the tone of
the prologue: "ennemi secret," "faux plaisirs,"
"maux," "chimeres," "voluptez monsongeres," "vaine
douceur," etc. And whereas Henri is the benevo-

lent prince (in the prose), Love is the unmerciful
tyrant. Thus the reader is equally aware of a
juxtaposition in every line of the poem of opposite terms--symbolizing perhaps the separation of
the signifier and the expected signified--one term
denoting pleasure, the other affliction. In the
first line, for example, the most tender and deli-
cate of human sentiments, Love, abruptly becomes a
villainous tyrant; secret enemy is juxtaposed with
prosperity in the second line; pleasures are
qualified as false; ecstasy ("voluptez") is
designated as deceptive ("mensongeres"), and so
forth throughout the maxim.

Maxim I is thus anticipatory; for in spite
of the promise that the king's coronation may have
evoked, one suspects now that passion will take
possession of the new ruler's soul with regret-
table consequences. However, it is not the loves
and misfortunes of Henri III that will constitute
the core of this first prose segment. In spite of
the orientation of the nouvelle up to this point,
one will not read how the monarch's reason is
seduced ("en seduisant les sens") nor how his
heart is destroyed ("amolissent le coeur") by this
tyrannical passion. In fact the king's "story" is
briefly summarized and is mentioned only insofar
as it relates to the lives of the principal
characters: the duc de Guise and a certain Mme de
Sauve. It is through their personalities that one
will see the effects of Love; through their destinies, the reader will witness the unfolding of
each line of the maxim as it assumes its full
meaning. One will indeed see the key words and
phrases of the maxim repeated and transformed
throughout the development of the plot.

Mme de Sauve, one of the king's mistresses,
is first presented to the reader as the most
charming lady in all of France. The power of her
beauty is far-reaching and unequivocal. But this
magnificent exterior belies her contemptible
character; for she seems to be, in this nouvelle,
the embodiment of the appearance-versus-reality
dichotomy. Yet she is hardly unique or the
exception; all of the historical characters tend
to hide their true selves behind deceiving public
masks. The "honest" King of Navarre, for example,
consents to *feign* interest in Mme de Sauve in

order to gain the favors of one of her enemies; while, simultaneously, Mme de Sauve herself has been instructed by the queen mother (for political purposes) to *pretend* to be accepting favorable the king's advances.

The result is that both Navarre and Mme de Sauve--each unaware of the other's true sentiments and motives--are *pretending* to be in love. Here, the sign (the public mask) becomes a means of con-cealing the truth. During the course of these pretenses, Navarre actually does fall in love with Mme de Suave (his passion for the first object of his desire evaporates completely--see Appendix A). He conducts himself, nevertheless, as though he were still enchanted with his former mistress (a dissimulation); and although he confesses his love to his new mistress, he continues to *pretend* to be only pretending to love in the presence of her enemies (a dissimulation of a dissimulation).

But this proves to be only the beginning of the dissimulations. In another intrigue, Mme de Sauve affects a tone of reconcilation with her former lover, the duc de Guise, in whom she has no real interest. Guise himself, who is completely duped by her lies, proposes, for political reasons, that he and Mme de Sauve *hide* their reconciliation and that they continue feigning discord before the court members. Unaware of Mme de Sauve's malicious intentions, he considers him-self the happiest of all lovers.

Thus in the first prose segment of the nouvelle, the "disorders" which are the result of this schism between appearance and reality, affect life only in the inner court circles. This is perhaps best symbolized by the disorders and con-fusion in the court ballet, which by definition, is the essence of order: ART.[8]

The second half of this nouvelle begins with *Maxime II*:

Mais est-il un bon-heur effectif et durable,
Dans ce qui roule sur l'Amour?
Tout s'y trouve suject aux perils d'un retour;

Son espoir le plus juste & le plus vraisembliable,
Nait, se détruit, & renait dans un jour.
Ses douceurs passent comme un songe,
Ses promesses ne sont qu'un seduisant mensonge;
Et toutesfois, ô triste aveuglement!
Ce que nous connoissons de plus grand sur la
*   terre,*
Ce qui fait à nos yeux son plus bel ornement,
Les loix, l'honneur, la paix, la guerre,
Tout se trouve sujet à son enchantment!

What is enunciated in the first part of this nouvelle as the duc de Guise's happiness is now a "faux plaisir" and a "volupté mensongère." Guise's destiny is darkened by an ominous cloud in the form of the rhetorical question of this second maxim: "Is there a true and lasting joy in matters of love?" And whereas in the first part of this nouvelle the disorders are confined to court activity, henceforth the disruptions caused by passion will infiltrate and ultimately encompass the entirety of the political and religious life in France. In this second prose segment, the reader can again see each verse of the maxim expand and develop into the plot as he follows Mme de Sauve and the duke's love.

Here, too, there are key words that will color and guide the "reading" of history: "songe," "mensonge," "aveuglement," etc. The reader will observe Love, forever blinding, crystallize, die, and be re-born within a brief interval. He will recognize the promises of lovers to be merely seductive lies ("séduisant mensonge") and all that French civilization values and honors to be subject to Love's bewitchment.

Maxime III

Que de malheurs, presens ou preparez,
Accompagnent toujours, l'Amour & sa manie;
Que de maux nous causa ce trait de jalousie,
Et qu'il fallut de temps pour les voir reparez!
Fatale passion, enchantement des âmes,
Ah! que le ciel étoit irrité contre nous,
Quand on y vit écrit que tes funestes flames,

Auroient pour nos desirs quelque chose de doux.

The *bon-heur* of the first line of the second maxim modulates here into an irrevocable *malheur, maux,* and *manie.* In constrast with the first and second maxims which are in the present tense denoting the universal truths of the statements, this final poem is, for the most part, in the past tense (aorist). This becomes significant in light of Benveniste's formulation of the definition of *récit historique*: it is through the registering of an event in the temporal and historical mode of expression that it becomes past, historical. By enunciating the consequences of passion in the aorist, Mme de Villedieu establishes them as fact, inscribes them into history.

With the exception of the first two lines which are in the present tense, this final maxim does not so much affirm a general truth as it constitutes then a projection and a historization of the plot: jealousy over Mme de Sauve *did cause* France much internal anguish and internal disorders ("Que de maux nous *causa* ce trait de jalousie"--the emphasis on the verb added); it *created* the animosity between the King of Navarre and the duc de Guise; it *caused* the king's brother to ally himself with the Protestants of Germany; *it precipitated* disorders within the royal family, etc. In brief, it was passion that laid the foundations for the civil strife that for years eviscerated the kingdom. The narrator concludes by restating the lesson with which he began--"*Que l'Amour est le ressort de toutes les autres passions de l'âme*"--thus closing the nouvelle in a circular motion that seems to give it a certain impenetrable and inalterable finality.[9]

The first "disorders" caused by passion, as an analysis of plot reveals, appear in the characters' language: words are no longer bearers of a "truth"; gestures and expressions conceal instead of reveal. And as a result, communication degenerates into confusion as the "sign" can no longer be "trusted." It is this disruption in the linguistic *order* that leads to the disorders in the private lives of the court members and subsequently to those of an entire nation.

63

Symbolically, in the nouvelle, there are two episodes of intercepted letters, where the addresser/addressee chain and the communication process are broken.[10] Moreover, it is equally significant that the only way that Guise is able to challenge the "power" of his mistress, the only means by which he can be forceful and even threatening is by means of the written word. When he can no longer withstand Mme de Sauve's *présence*, the letter becomes a substitute for the duke himself; he invests it with the power that he is lacking.

But it is especially in the second nouvelle that one will see further how Love, by perverting first the communication process, leads to other disorders and crimes.

Nouvelle II

The problem posed in the second nouvelle concerns that of the sign, not pre-eminently in its vertical composition (the relationship between signifier and signified), but rather the problem of the sign in its horizontal extension. That is to say, it is a question of the sign in its inter-action with other signs: the problem of dis-course.[11] Viewed in its horizontal "connection," the question is no longer specifically that of (visual) representation (appearance versus reality) but rather that of communication, the exchange of signs between two subjects.[12] In this perspective, one is no longer as much concerned with appearance and reality as one is with the question of code, contact, encoder, and decoder of a specific message.

The second nouvelle is punctuated in two places by intervening maxims in verse and it is somewhat more unevenly divided than the first story. The nouvelle commences with the following *sententia* or subtitle: *"Qu'on ne peut donner si peu de puissance à l'amour qu'il n'en abuse."*

And, as in the first nouvelle, this proves to constitute the essence of the story reduced to its simplest form.

If, in the first *Exemple* (term employed by Mme de Villedieu) of love's disorders, the political and civil disorders germinate from or perhaps reflect a malfunction in the linguistic realm, here too they stem from a kind of linguistic disorder. For the historical characters in this second nouvelle, it is the communication process itself--addresser/addressee, context/contact, message/code--that is perverted (see Appendix B). This usually assumes one of several forms in the text where the addresser/addressee's contact is severed: intercepted letters; disequilibrated conversations (either because of the *silence* or total absence of one of the interlocutors, or because of the surreptitious presence of an "illegitimate" listener who overhears the conversations and espies the actions of others). And if in the first example passions invade and corrupt the political order, here political ambition reciprocally invades and disrupts the world of love.

The second story, like the first, begins on an optimistic note; the heroic atmosphere appears even more pronounced: the Marquis de Termes marries a young provincial woman simply because it is convenient. He discovers, much to his surprise, that she possesses "une beauté parfaite" and more "esprit de politesse" than is usual for one of her status so that love, which does not precede the marriage, is born after their union. But in a very essential way this union proves extremely difficult to "consummate." Mme de Termes, tortured by some dark secret (and ignoring her husband's supplications, orders, and threats, in his attempt to penetrate the mystery), remains silent; or when she does speak, it is never the truth. Broken down ultimately by the tactics of her husband, however, the marquise relinquishes and tells M. de Termes what he wishes so to know: she reveals the existence of her violent and eternal passion for M. de Termes' nephew, the baron de Bellegarde.

This confession appears to possess all the

characteristics of a true heroic act; and Mme de Termes seems rather close to the Cornelian Pauline as she is torn between her love and her duty[13]:

> Cependant, puisque vous me forcez à vous l'avoüer, moins je le voi [le baron] & plus je sens le desir de le voir. . .& jugeant de ses peines par les miennes, il se fait en moi un combat de pitié, d'amour & de devoir, qui semble dechirer mon ame, & dont les effects sont si cruels pour elle, que de quelque côté que panche la victoire, elle me sera toujours également funeste. (p. 72)

Such a rare confession as this naturally pierces the husband with such an ineffable pain, writes the narrator, that he is rendered *speechless* and finally has to flee these oppressive words. After a few days reflection, M. de Termes attempts once again to *speak* to his wife. This proves to be the couple's first true conversation--one where there is a genuine verbal exchange. It is, however, their final one as well; for the marquis renounces at this point his "interlocutory" rights as her husband (he vows never again to attempt to speak to her).

Thus, in the first part of this nouvelle, the couple's first two conversations or attempts at verbal "intercourse" are incomplete and unfulfilled. In the first instance, the wife refuses to converse, to surrender her "words"; and in the second, when she does speak, it is a false discourse. When Mme de Termes is finally able to confess openly and honestly and the couple is able to enjoy a genuine verbal exchange, it results in the death of the husband: first symbolically in the form of mutism and then quite literally on the battle field.

It is at this point that Mme de Villedieu places *Maxime IV*:

Mais helas! il ne faut que donner à l'amour
Un léger droit, d'étaler son language:
Ce premier pas, dans l'ame la plus sage,
L'expose à se voir quelque jour

Soûmise toute entiere aux effets de sa rage.
Jamais, aux coeurs bien nez, il ne se laisse voir
Qu'apparemment soûmis aux regles du devoir.
C'est la vertus, dit-il qui l'anime & l'engage;
Sans elle il ne seroit qu'une ardeur de passage.
A-t-il, sous ce masque trompeur,
Pris quelque pied dedans un jeune coeur,
Il en bannit toute l'horreur du crime.
La vertus, la raison, le desir pour l'estime,
La bien-seance & la pudeur,
Tout devient tôt ou tard la mourante victime
De cet impitoyable & rusé suborneur.

Maxim IV is an elaboration of the subtitle of this nouvelle; it surpasses in fact the form of a maxim properly speaking as it is here that the introductory *sententia* is transformed into a *reflection.*[14] Moreover, it is a reprise and an expansion of the final four verses of Maxim II: "Ce que nous connoissons de plus grand sur la terre/Ce qui fait à nos yeux son plus bel ornement,/Les loix, l'honneur, la paix, la guerre/Tout se trouve sujet à son enchantement." As the story unfolds, each line of verse is again expanded and transformed to comprise the elements of the plot. Thus two very noble souls, because of love, will suffer all of its rages ("soûmise toute entiere aux effets de sa rage"). Under the guise of duty and virtue, the disorders of passion will manifest themselves ("il ne se laisse voir/Qu'apparemment soûmis aux regles du devoir"). For the young baron as well as for his mistress, this passion will render even criminal acts acceptable ("il en bannit toute l'horreur du crime").

The second part of the nouvelle begins with *Maxime V*:

Mais Felicité Mensongere
Votre illusion passagere
N'a pas si tôt paru, qu'elle s'évanouit
Le bonheur des amans est tout dans l'esperance
Ce qui de loin les éblouit
Perd de prés son éclat et sa fausse apparence;
Et tel mettoit un plus haut prix
A la felicité si long-tems desirée,
Qui la trouve à son gré plus digne de mépris,
Quand avec son espoir il l'a bien comparée.

Maxim V is equally the reprise and expansion of maxims I and II; and, indeed, the entire fifth maxim functions as a response to the intitial question of the second one: "Mais est-il un bonheur effectif et durable/Dans ce qui roule dans l'Amour?"

I remarked above that in the first part of this nouvelle the "interlocutory marriage" between M. de Termes and his wife is extremely diffult to consummate. In the second part, where Mme de Termes becomes Mme de Bellegarde, one will see essentially the same process. In fact, the remainder of the nouvelle can be characterized as a *thématique refusée*: that of the unrealized and unrealizable "conversation" between the baron de Bellegarde and his new wife. As a result, the text is comprised essentially of one scene which is transformed and repeated (with intervening explanations to situate it) without ever being fully actualized.[15] The scene takes the form of aborted conversations, dialogues by means of an intermediary, the schism of the addressee/ addresser in intercepted correspondences, and overheard conversations.[16] Though the scene varies, the verbal exchange between the spouses in each of these instances is somehow prevented and perverted. Each scene, therefore, lacks one essential element that would make it a true exchange:

("Silence of the listener"): In the first instance Bellegarde is besieged by his wife's verbal abuses ("elle lui fit des pièces si sanglantes") as she has reason to complain of his apparent disinterest in her. Confused and not knowing how to respond to these allegations, the baron avoids all conversation with his wife. Unable to elicit a response from her husband, Mme de Bellegarde resorts to surreptitious means to discover his thoughts and motives. This she accomplishes with an unusual amount of success; but in the process, she loses all personal (i.e., verbal) contact with him and thus she has no way to communicate her own position to him. It is in order to do this that Mme de Bellegarde uses the queen mother as a kind of "go-between", and it is only with the queen as their contact that they communicate. (While Mme de Bellegarde has been intercepting her husband's letters, he has been writing others in her name--counterfeit messages--designed to discredit her and to put her reputation into question. In effect, he forges a kind of "conversation" between his wife and an alleged lover.) (See Appendix B)

("Surreptitious presence of an 'illegitimate' listener"): In the very last instance where the spouses meet face to face, again, they never seem able to speak directly to each other. He conceals himself so as to overhear one of her conversations, and when he does reveal himself, he is confronted by such a (verbally) strong, vindictive, and imperturbable wife that once more he is reduced to a state of *speechlessness*.

The narrator concludes this nouvelle as he* does the first by paraphrasing the maxim that serves as its subtitle: "*Qu'on ne peut donner si peu de puissance à l'amour qu'il n'en abuse*," again ending the story with an unchallengeable finality. The narrator seems confident that there is no leeway for a further elaboration or for a different interpretation of the events of history.

He also ties this second example of the disorders of love to the first by restating here the introductory *sententia* of the first story: "Que l'Amour est le ressort de toutes les passions de l'ame." This narrative regression, in a manner of speaking, confirms that the relationship between these two stories resembles that of concentric circles, the first enclosing the second.

---

*I am of course making the distinction here between Mme de Villedieu, the author, and the narrator within the story. Whereas the textual evidence seems to support the contention that the narrator (*narratrice*) in *La Princesse de Clèves*, for example, is feminine (see R. Francillon, *L'Oeuvre Romanesque de Mme de Lafayette*, pp. 206-214), this is not the case for *Les Désordres de l'Amour*. Quite the contrary, one is forced, I believe, to attribute a masculine "posture" to its narrator.

(Chronologically, the events of the second nouvelle can be situated between two of the events of the first.)

In this second nouvelle, as in the first, the two maxims fragment the prose at strategic points and serve therefore as a guide in the reading of history. That is to say, they appear precisely at those points in the story where the narrator perceives that the reader, relying on the previously accepted "historical" (i.e., political) explanations, might possibly question the narrator's "passional" interpretation of these events. Both of these poems are written entirely in the present tense and are thereby conspicuous both as infractions of the temporal sequence and as verse. Yet the relationship between these two maxims and their narrative expansions seems less strict or precise than in the first nouvelle. The aphorisms are now more general and abstract. They offer comments less on the specifics of the particular historical events in question than they do on human nature and passion in general. This is to say that the *narrative* element or function of the verse has been reduced. The expansion of the maxims does not yield uniquely this *particular* story (as is the case with the relationship between the first three maxims and the prose into which they are expanded); the maxims in this nouvelle could now be expanded to produce a number of similar stories.

In the first nouvelle, for example, the intervening maxims could only have been presented in the particular order and at the precise instant at which they occur, as the verse follows closely the development of the plot. In this second nouvelle, on the contrary, the two maxims, though still occuring at stragetic points, are practically interchangeable and could conceivably have been positioned in the reverse order without affecting the reading of the story or the role of the maxims in its interpretation.

The third and fourth nouvelles, which in effect constitute a single story, comprise about one-half of Mme de Villedieu's 1675 text. From the problem of the sign in the first nouvelle to that of verbal discourse or intercourse in the second, one might metaphorically speak of these last nouvelles in terms of the problematic of the literary text, the *scriptum*. As in Mme de Villedieu's first example of love's disorders, it is a question of appearance versus reality. Here, there are two very different and distinct configurations--on the one hand, human activity and on the other, human psychology or motivation-- that are presented as superficial structure and deep structure respectively whose relationship must be specified. And, as in the second nouvelle, one again encounters the problems of the encoder and decoder of a certain message and their relationship or contact.

In the first two stories, war, peace, life, death, and honor all depend on love; and just as the greatest works of nature (in the persons of the duc de Guise, M. de Termes, Mme de Sauve, and Mme de Bellegarde) are destroyed or become destructive due to the "malfeasance" of love, so too in this last story is one of the greatest works of art, poetry, a possible cause and effect of this disrupting passion. The emphasis on the *verbum* of the first two nouvelles--conversations and letters (or "written conversations")--shifts to a focus on literary discourse. Indeed, as predicted in the maxim of the first nouvelle, everything that civilization values is subject to love's enchantment.

This last story, in the manner of the preceding ones, begins with a *sententia*: "*Qu'il n'y a point de desespoir où l'amour ne soit capable de jetter un homme bien amoureux.*" Moreover, the same elements with which the other stories are constructed and which constitute their thematic-- letters and conversations--reappear here in varying forms. These include counterfeit letters, anonymous messages, overheard conversations, and disequilibrated dialogues (see Appendix C).

71

("The Lost Letters/The Found Meaning"): The first part of this story (or *Exemple III* according to the divisions of the text) concerns Givry d'Anglure, his mistress (the beautiful Mme de Maugiron) and her rival, the equally beautiful and "talented", princesse de Guise. On the surface Givry appears to possess everything: he is handsome and most importantly he possesses the love of his mistress with whom he spends many hours "en de douces conversations." Moreover, her confessions of love are unequivocal and unabashed, and when forced to be separated from her, Givry receives such tender and intimate love letters that they succeed in consoling him during her absence. During the course of a military campaign, Givry loses these prized possessions; they fall into the hands of the enemy. This constitutes a kind of symbolic loss which slowly transforms itself into a real one as the hero loses in fact Mme de Maugiron's love. When these letters reappear they have undergone a kind of re-composition (*ré-écriture*); each one contains a poem (written in "un chractère inconnu," p.125) inscribed on the verso.

In constrast with the first two stories where the maxims punctuate and divide the stories into "parts," here, they appear as a group.[17] In terms of the narrative progression, the focus of the third nouvelle is twofold: first, to identify the author of the verses and the circumstances surrounding their composition (the motives of the poet); and, secondly, to specify their meaning *vis à vis* the content of the letters. Mlle de Guise is quickly identified as the poet; and whereas the meaning of the poetry in relation to the letters eventually becomes clear to Givry, the princess' motivation for composing them remains a mystery. The effect of the verses, however, is immediate: they unleash Givry's passion; he becomes henceforth obsessed with their author; but as she is a great princess, he dares not confess his passion, *speak* his love. Furthermore, he no longer finds in his mistress' (Mme de Maugiron's) letters or even in her conversations any charm or pleasure. Now, whenever she confesses her intimate and tender sentiments, Givry recalls the poem in which Mlle de Guise condemns excessive expressions of love. He even assures the young princess that her verses have dissipated the "blindness of his heart" ("Givry avoit assuré la jeune princesse que les vers qu'elle lui avoit envoyez avoient dissipé l'aveuglement de son coeur ..." p. 159). They make evident to him that which is hidden; they demystify his present affair.

Although within the context of the nouvelle the maxims apply specifically to Givry's relationship with Mme de Maugiron, the reader recognizes that they apply equally to the entire plot for they summarize what is to follow. Mlle de Guise composes these verses, for example, as evidence of her "finesse d'esprit et delicatesse de coeur" (p. 136), but they constitute in reality only "des caprices d'humeur" *(Maxime VI)*. Moreover, *Maxime VIII*, a repetition and development of several of the maxims from the preceding stories, will be particularized and rendered explicit in the present story both in Mme de Maugiron's irrational and tyrannical passion for Givry and the latter's equally irrational and unrealistic love for Mlle de Guise. And, as the final maxim indeed suggests will be the case, Givry's initial pleasure and joy in Mme de Maugiron's company ("le doux tems de la joie") is merely a fleeting and exhaustible happiness; and, for Mme de Maugiron, in spite of her commiserating supplications and reprimands, love proves to be a pleasure irretrievably lost ("il faut. . .compter pour perdu tout moment qu'on emploie en des reproches superflus"--*Maxime IX*).

("The False Letter/The Sound Meaning"): The second half of this story (or the fourth nouvelle) displays no intervening poetic maxim. In terms of the plot, the *lost* letters in the first part modulate into the *false* letter of the second, as someone has sent a daring and inappropriate confession of love to the princesse de Guise in Givry's name. This message insults and provokes the princess' anger. And althought the letter is forged or counterfeit, its contents, its message *per se* is *sound* or legitimate for it does articulate eloquently and communicate effectively Givry's innermost sentiments, the passion he himself dares not verbalize. As is the case with Mlle de Guise's poems, certain questions arise: who is the author of the letter, what are the circumstances surrounding its composition?; once more attention is drawn to the effects of the message: it incites the princess' passion for Bellegarde (the letter's true author).

In preferring Mlle de Guise to Mme de Maugiron, in going from the prolix confessions of the latter to the restrained verses of the former, Givry in effect foresakes the *verbum* for the *scriptum,* a real passion for a phantom hope. For after the incident of the letter, Mlle de Guise treats Givry with an indignant *silence.* In addition, in the presence of the princess, the hero himself is often speechless; whereas with Mme de Maugiron, he speaks sincerely and coldly of the death of his passion for her.

When the hero later refuses to respond to Mme de Maugiron (at first he chooses not to answer her letters and, finally even her verbal supplications reach a deaf ear), she, like Mme de Termes-Bellegarde of the second nouvelle, resorts to spying and eavesdropping. Significantly and symbolically, the only letter that Givry can find enough courage to write to the princess, his death letter, is one where the addresser/addressee's contact is non-existent and where the message can never be communication.

This final example of the disorders of love, and with it the entire text of Mme de Villedieu, concludes with a poem:

> *Amour, cruel amour, enchantement des ames,*
> *Helas! ne verrons-nous jamais*
> *Le funeste effet de tes flames*
> *Respecter dans nos coeurs la sagesse & la*
> *Paix.*

These concluding verses are projected towards an impossible utopia, symbolized perhaps in the future form of the verb ("voir") and its negative modality, where the malefactions and ravages of passion would succumb to the order and peace of reason. From the examples of human nature documented, it is suggested that this is indeed an unobtainable state; for underneath the beautiful

and illustrious exteriors of the characters lurk
an inherent weakness and blindness. Instead of
being the masters of their own actions and thus of
their own fates, the important historical figures
exist at the mercy of their passions. These irrational, involuntary, and ubiquitous forces determine their every act and dominate their every
thought.[18]

** ** **

In the progression from the first to the
second nouvelle, I have shown how one can perceive
a slight change in the function of the poetic
maxim. What I have referred to as the "narrative"
elements of the verses (the maxim as *mini-récit*)
appear less obvious. In the first story, as indicated above, the expansion or narrative development of the maxims would produce invariably and
uniquely the story of Henri III or rather, that of
the duc de Guise and Mme de Sauve--the series of
historical events that occurred in France at that
specific time. In the second, though the prose is
still an exemplification of the verse, the maxims
appear not to be applicable uniquely to the events
in question, that is to say, the story of Mme de
Termes-Bellegarde and her husbands. In the last
two nouvelles this shift is completed. Here, the
maxims have all but lost their specific narrative
connection with the prose. Although the fundamental relationship maxim/prose remains exactly the
same, the narrative expansion of the aphorisms
would indeed "yield" an almost infinite number of
"similar" stories. Thus the maxims here can very
nearly be compared to a generative grammar in the
sense that they constitute somewhat a "system of
rules that can iterate to generate an indefinitely
large number of structures."[19]

Significantly, in these last two divisions
of Mme de Villedieu's text, the maxims in verse
are presented, not as interventions of the
narrating agent, but as the *literary productions*

of one of the protagonists. They appear no longer as positions of a discursive code (exegesis) but as part of the narrative configuration itself (diegesis). They constitute the "text," in a manner of speaking, of the heroine (as poet) who occupies the privileged position of being able to perceive and to analyze the events that comprise her present, much as the narrator (and therefore the reader) is in a comparable position to observe and to analyze them as past occurrences.

Finally, it has been my observation that the moral and political disorders in Mme de Villedieu's nouvelles invariably stem from a problem in communication, a problem of language. To elaborate further: Love, perhaps in the manner of the Original Sin, is the germ, the malefactor, the cause of the characters' deplorable state; and the first sign of this corruption surfaces symptomatically in their language. This particular passion has a deleterious and disruptive effect on their linguistic system which ultimately affects their emotional, religious, political, and social systems as well. Since it disorients all thought, it *dis*-orders all speech, all action. Through a kind of false language love arouses exaggerated expectations of pleasure[20] ("Mais helas! il ne faut que donner à l'amour/Un leger droit, d'étaler son langage. . . Mais Le bonheur des amans est tout dans l'esperance")--thus the false discourse of a Mme de Sauve or of a princesse de Guise and the "faux plaisir" and the "voluptez mensongeres" of a duc de Guise or of a Givry. It is language that necessarily crystallizes and disseminates the disorders for, inalterably, each character's conception of truth or reality is founded upon the others' "faux discours"; from such false discourses, he forms false impressions; from these false impressions, he makes false judgments; and these false judgments result in inappropriate actions that bring about disastrous and irrevocable consequences.[21]

THE MAXIM AS "OPERATIVE FORCE"
WITHIN THE NOUVELLE

In diagramming what can be metaphorically referred to as the "kernel sentences" of her text and then in using these moral principles as her point of departure, has not the novelist weakened her narration by rendering it too predictable and perhaps even boring?[22] Quite obviously the maxims are anticipatory; for indeed they do lessen somewhat the impact of the stories in preparing, for example, the reader to observe many of the most celebrated souls in French history in an unflattering light and in a way that shows how little they resemble the Classical *généreux*. There is a certain complicity between the narrator and the reader; for it is in part through the poetic maxims that the latter knows more or less what the characters themselves do not know and that he can see clearly the faults of the characters' actions, the fallacies in their reasoning. Yet the nouvelles are not totally predictable, nor are they boring; for as Cuénin points out in her introduction, Mme de Villedieu still surprises the reader by introducing the "unforeseeable." One example will illustrate this: on three different occasions in the first nouvelle, plots arise against Mme de Sauve that each time nearly provoke her exile, but on each occasion unexpected circumstances (that prove indeed to be "historical") intervene at the last possible minute as reprieves.

Much in the same way, writes Cuénin, as the reader follows the destinies of the main characters in this same nouvelle, the maxims do not suspend his interest in the story's development nor do they minimize the suspense of the plot. This nouvelle does not reach its climax until after the second maxim when the two lovers, blinded by a superficial tranquillity, witness the dissipation of their good fortune. In effect, apropos of their mercurial love relationship, practically every paragraph ends in dramatic suspense. Moreover, it is in part this suspense or this dramatic quality in the nouvelle which

77

distinguishes it from the historical source from which it is inspired.

The position of the maxims in the text underscores the didactic presentation of the historical characters and facts: the selection of the historical "materials" is dictated by the purpose of the example to be demonstrated. They indicate, therefore, the organization of a specific discourse in relation to the events related. This obviously must be an implication of the enunciator, in this case, the narrator. Since these aphoristic verses also contain, in a compact and economical form, a seemingly full grasp of the historical facts and relevant issues, they point to a narrator who has assumed a certain position and distance in relation to the events and who has full command over their recall. They suggest, therefore, that a single vision or critical perspective will filter and color the narrated events.

But since the maxims are enunciated outside of and separate from the "text" *stricto sensu*-- that is to say that the nouvelles would remain coherent, unified and artistically complete were the maxims to be suppressed--one could conclude that these organizing principles, insofar as they explain the "why's" of the plot and the motives of the characters, are neither unique nor intrinsic to the particular events in question; nor perhaps would they be immediately obvious or apparent in a pure "representation" (history/prose). Instead they would likely remain hidden for the uninitiated spectator (in this instance the reader) just as they are perhaps unconscious for the protagonists. In this sense, it is the maxims that accord *order*, i.e., comprehension, to the seeming *disorder* of human activity in general and political activity in particular.

It is in part through the un-integrated maxim, therefore, that the narrative voice presents, almost parenthetically, the moral "causes" which permit the reader to understand fully the particular political and social "effects" under consideration and which simultaneously allow him to transcend the particularities of these individual situations. So the maxims serve also to universalize the lessons of the plots. They reveal,

of course, that the narrator has a particular perception and understanding of the politics and of
the situations presented that lead him to the
discovery of some timeless laws of human behavior.

What is presented on one level as the discontinuity and the elements of confusion in
history (war, peace, revolutions, etc.) is
explained on another in terms of the laws or the
continuity of human nature. This seems to suggest
that the past (history) has no coherence, meaning,
or order except by virtue of that given to it by
the present discourse. (Symbolically, just as
passions disrupt the continuity of political and
social life, so too the maxim disrupts the continuity of the prose nouvelle.) This continuity
of human passions is atemporal (evidenced by the
present tense) since it is bound by no particular
time period. Thus the maxims can be said to fluc-
tuate between the past of the narrated event and
the present and future of the linguistic event,
the moment of discourse. It is characterized by
the time of the *one who is relating* and constitutes consequently one of the (explicit) shifters
that marks the passage from *énoncé* to *énonciation*.

The maxims are thus esthetic devices through
which the author establishes a narrator/reader
duality or interchange. Esthetic devices,
however, may conceal epistemological assumptions
especially if they are incorporated into a system
where a moral code is expounded: "What in one
author may be a literary method introduced to vary
the texture of the narrative may in another become
an epistemological statement about the materials
of truth itself."[23] The use of the maxim as a
hidden order (poetry) that must be extracted from
a surface disorder (prose) reflects a similar view
in the relationship between (conscious) actions
and (unconscious) motives. Human behavior, as
manifested in the historical events, is a surface
structure or articulation that must somehow be
re-translated or reduced to its deeper signification.

It is interesting to recall again and to
explore further the fact that as one progresses
from the first to the third nouvelle, the poetic
maxims which begin as "extra-textual" or *hors-*

textes (and which remain so in a strictly formal sense or as far as the form *per se* of the text is concerned) become, superficially at least, absorbed by and incorporated into the text. For if the status or function that the maxim fulfills in Mme de Villedieu's text is not immediately obvious, it becomes so in the last story: just as it is only after a "re-reading" of his love letters in conjunction with Mlle de Guise's poetry (this *ré-écriture*) that Givry can understand them --that their true meaning becomes accessible or that he is able to transcend the surface articulation to grasp the deep structure--so too must history be re-read in a particular perspective for its meaning to surface. In other words, the maxims in the third nouvelle function on two different levels: on the one hand, they are part of the *récit* since they influence or motivate the events of history; on the other hand, they constitute a part of the *discours* which assigns a meaning to the events. In the first instance, they are addressed directly to the historical reader (Givry); in the second, they are addressed indirectly to the assumed reader of the nouvelle. Moreover, when the enunciator of the maxims is transformed into a character in the story, the character becomes a kind of metaphor for the interpretative act, the *discours*, while remaining intrinsically a part of the *récit*.

Yet the attempt to include these extra-textual elements (*hors-textes*) into the text does not alter the fundamental narrator/reader configuration. But the presentation of the poetic aphorisms as the commentary of one of the actors in the story as opposed to that of a mediating voice detached and separate from it would seem to have an important implication for the presentation of the story: it "objectifies" and reinforces the narrator's position within the text by transposing these discursive elements into narrative ones.

In a slightly different perspective, when the author of the maxim is implicated in the action, the historical problems presented are posed in terms of a certain immediacy. The past is generally considered the place of the example, the lesson; but the present can be so as well. In a sense, the "he" of the historical event (*énoncé*) can assume the position of the "I" of the literary event (*énonciation*). It is in part for this reason that in the final nouvelle the historical characters appear no longer as mere (literary) objects manipulated by an omniscient narrator who analyzes and condemns them from a distance, but they appear somewhat as (historical) "subjects" capable of identifying and assessing their own passions.[24]

Mme de Villedieu postulates nothing new when she affirms that personal and individual passions influence the events of history, for the seventeenth-century historian would suggest as much. In Mme de Villedieu's text (as has been shown to be the case in *La Princesse de Clèves* as well), these personal causes and passions do not always imply a conscious exercise of will; her characters become lost in the labyrinth of their own words, thoughts, and actions. As the seventeenth-century writer had no way to articulate the unconscious, Mme de Villedieu perhaps represents it symbolically in this mixed genre of prose and verse.[25]

NOTES

PART II CHAPTER TWO

1. See notes 8 and 9 of Introduction, pp. 10, 11.

2. Again, I employ the term "shifter" in the sense that Jakobson gives it as an "overlapping of message and code" and more specifically as parts of the code referring to the message:

> Any linguistic code contains a particular class of units which Jespersen labeled SHIFTERS: the general meaning of a shifter cannot be defined without a reference to the message.
>
> Their semiotic nature was discussed by Burks* in his study on Peirce's classification of signs into symbols, indices, and icons. According to Peirce, a symbol (e.g. the English word *red*) is associated with the represented object by a conventional rule, while the index (e.g. the act of pointing) is in existential relation with the object it represents. Shifters combine both functions and belong therefore to the class of INDEXICAL SYMBOLS. As a striking example Burks cites the personal pronoun. "I" means the person uttering "I." Thus on the one hand, the sign "I" cannot represent its object without being associated with the latter "by a conventional rule," and in different codes the same meaning is assigned to different sequences such as *I, ego, ich, ja,* etc.: consequently "I" is a symbol. On the other hand, the sign "I" cannot represent its object without "being in existential relation" with this object: the word "I" designating the utterer is existentially

---

*A. W. Burks, "Icon, Index, and Symbol," *Philosophy and Phenomenological Research,* IX (1949).

related to his utterance, and hence functions as an index. . .

("Shifters, Verbal Categories, and the Russian
Verb," *Selected Works*, pp. 131-132.)

3. Benveniste, p. 244.

4. The paradox here is in reality only a superficial one. For if it is, as I have just
affirmed, the intervention and the *presence* of the
narrator in the text that constitute the shifter,
then this withdrawal would constitute a kind of
"non-shifter." Yet, as will be shown later in
this discussion, this very *absence* reveals much,
if not more, about the position of the narrator
vis à vis his text.

5. This curious mixture of prose and verse was
indeed *à la mode* during Mme de Villedieu's day.
The four editions of the collection of poetry
published by Sercy between 1660 and 1663 include a
number of texts where there is a combination of
prose and verse. Micheline Cuénin in her introduction to *Les Désordres de l'Amour* lists many
other examples of the popularity of such texts.
In 1664, for example, A. de Sommaville published a
*Nouveau Mélange de pièces curieuses tant en
prose qu'en vers*; and around 1663 (Sercy) there
appeared *Recueil des Portraits en vers et prose*.
Mme de Villedieu herself published in 1660
(Barbin) the enormously successful *Le Récit en
prose et en vers de la fable des Précieuses* and
in 1671 appeared her *Oeuvres Mêlées*. This same
mixture can be found to some extent in her *Journal
Amoureux* (1669), *Anaxandre* (1667), and *Lisandre*
(1663).

La Fontaine mixed prose and verse in *Songe de
Vaux*--fragments of which appeared in 1665 and in
1671--and in a short prose work entitled *Les
Amours de Psyché et de Cupidon* (1669).

Moreover, the four-volume *Recueil des pièces
galantes en prose et en vers* (Mme la comtesse de
la Suze) was in its sixth edition in 1674; and its
popularity apparently continued into the
eighteenth century, for in 1758 there were

eighteen editions. (See E. Magne, *Femmes Galantes du XVIIe Siècle, Mme de la Suze,* Mercure de France, 1908).

6. One has only to consider the influence and position of *L'Astrée* in seventeenth-century fiction.

7. I use "sign" here, not in its strict linguistic (Saussurean) acceptance, but in an extended and metaphorical sense. Inasmuch as the characters in this first nouvelle compose a society in which the task of each member is to "figure out" the others, to interpret the others, they constitute in a sense a system of (visual) signs. Each member appears as an enigma to be explained, as representative of something else to be deciphered. They wear public masks (signifiers) that reveal (or hide) an essence (signified).

Moreover, as will be seen in the second and third stories, it can be said, in a somewhat different perspective, that each member of this society emits material signs, both verbal and written, destined to produce an effect on the other members. In this sense I will speak of the characters, not so much as "signs" *representing*, but as "subjects" *communicating*. This, of course, does not constitute an absolute distinction for in all the stories the characters simultaneously stand for or represent something (visually) and communcate this something (verbally). It is rather a matter of the emphasis and the orientation of the particular nouvelle. In this first story this emphasis in placed on the effect of the physical presence of one member (who remains essentially expressionless and silent) on the others.

8. In order to celebrate the arrival of Paul, comte de Salmes, the king had instructed the royal house to invent "de nouveaux divertissemens." The Queen of Navarre assumed the responsibilities of creating a ballet for which Guise was to provide the choreography and which, according to their plans, was to be a mortal blow to Mme de Sauve's vanity. She was asked to dance as were other ladies of the court. The ballet was to represent the loves of Apollo and Daphne with the King of Navarre playing Apollo, Mlle de Châteauneuf as

Daphne, and Mme de Sauve as the hated Clitie.
Navarre was instructed to "marquer fortement ce
mépris, & à dire à Mme de Sauve," aprés le ballet,
que la fable étoit une vérité." But Navarre has
fallen in love with Mme de Sauve and resolves "de
faire tomber sur sa rivale la confusion qu'elle
lui avoit préparée:

> Il dissimula ce dessein jusqu'au jour que le
> ballet se dança, & comme on l'aprenoit & le
> repetoit toûjours à l'ordinaire, le Duc de
> Guise croyoit qu'il seroit executé comme il
> avoit été resolu. Il attendoit ce moment
> avec des impatiences extrêmes; . . . mais il
> fut bien surpris le jour du ballet quand il
> vit le Roi de Navarre faire le contraire de
> ce qu'on lui avoit proposé. Ce monarque
> commença par des excuses à Madame de Sauve,
> de ce que les personnages étoient si mal
> disposez; il lui dit ensuite que sa beauté
> étoit assez puissante pour renverser les
> ordres anciens & les modernes, & la suivant
> toutes les fois qu'il devoit la fuir, il mit
> tant de confusion dans *l'ordre* du
> ballet *qu'on ne sçut ce qu'il devoit repre-
> senter.*" (p. 24, emphasis added)

9.   I shall have occasion in Part Three of this
study to explore further this idea of the nouvelle
as a *final*, closed text.

10.   It is a question, of course, of the duc de
Guise's and Mme de Sauve's letters to each other.

11.   See note 7 above.

12.   I insist upon this emphasis on communcation,
signs, and the language of the characters in these
nouvelles because, from this, one can see how this
Classical writer envisioned the relationship between man and language. This in turn helps one to
understand her "artistic" approach to history;
for, as I shall suggest later, there are certain
parallels between her assumptions about the nature
of language and her assumptions about the nature
of the literary (i.e., poetic) text.

13. The character Pauline in Corneille's *Polyeucte* (1642) is often cited as the Cornelian heroine *par excellence*. It is her notion of honor and duty that determines her behavior. In the final analysis, however, it becomes clear that Mme de Termes is far from the heroic ideal because she is motivated, not by a real sense of esteem for and duty to her husband, but rather by a kind of self-serving *amour-propre*: she is, in fact, more concerned with her inability to marry her husband's nephew and her own possible unhappiness than she is with her husband's tranquillity (*"répos"*).

14. I am distinguishing here between the "maxim" and the "reflection" as related literary devices or genres where the second is a somewhat extended form of the first which, by definition, is usually short and limited. For an elaboration of the semantic distinction between the proverb, maxim, *pensée*, and reflection, see Sister Mary Francine Zeller's *New Aspects of Style in the Maxims of La Rochefoucauld* (Washington: The Catholic University Press, 1954), Chapter I: "The Maxim as a simple form and a literary genre--its History and Triumph."

15. Maurice Laugaa reveals a similar thematic in *La Princesse de Clèves* (*Lectures de Mme de Lafayette*, [Paris: Colin, 1971]).

16. The position and function of the "scene" in general, i.e., monologues, dialogues, in Mme de Villedieu's text will be the focus of Chapter Three of this study.

17. For these maxims, see Appendix D.

18. It is evident that Mme de Villedieu's work has been influenced by the Jansenist movement-- though not in a religious sense. Like La Rochefoucauld, the novelist subscribes to the negative view of human nature that is inherent in Jansenist thought. Her maxims, like his, reveal a total absence of confidence in man. But whereas for the Jansenists religion offers hope for man's redemption, for Mme de Villedieu there is no evidence of any such hope.

19.   Noam Chomsky, *Aspects of the Theory of Syntax* (Cambridge: The M.I.T. Press, 1965), pp. 15-16.

20.   Barbara Woshinsky, *La Princesse de Clèves: The Tension of Elegance* (The Hague: Mouton, 1973).

21.   Pierre Nicole writes: "Nos chutes viennent ordinairement de nos faux jugements, de nos fausses impressions; et nos fausses impressions, du commerce que nous avons les uns avec les autres par le langage. C'est la chaine malheureuse qui nous précipite dans l'enfer," (*Essais de Morale*, II, p. 57, quoted by B. Woshinsky, *La Princesse de Clèves*, p. 36.

22.   That is, "kernel sentence" as Chomsky describes: "These are sentences of a particularly simple sort that involve a minimum of transformational apparatus in their generation." (*Aspects of the Theory of Syntax*, pp. 17-18)

23.   Leo Braudy, *Narrataive Form in History and Fiction* (Princeton: Princeton University Press, 1970), p. 41.

24.   This, I think, will become clear after my discussion of the "integrated" shifter which follows and in which I shall trace the process whereby the characters become increasingly their own judges and analysts.

25.   B. Woshinsky makes similar claims for Mme de Lafayette's use of history and romance in *La Princesse de Clèves* (Chapter II: "History and Romance as Social Symbols").

CHAPTER THREE

THE EXEGETIC SHIFTER

From the beginning, then, the nouvelles are oriented toward an explicitly discursive end. I turn my attention now to the exegetic shifters that are integrated into the nouvelle and thus where the psychological and moral analysis, like the narrative itself, is in prose form. From these implicit or explicit signs within the text where the narrator "deposits" information about himself, his *contenance*, or his position *vis à vis* the narrated event, one begins to perceive further the narrating agent as a person, that is to say, as a pyschological and moral entity who expounds a personal position regarding the historical events and situations that he is narrating.

Periodically, then, the prose sections themselves of the nouvelles switch from *récit historique* to *discours* as the narrator functions both as a detached historian and as the analyst/moralist who comments and judges. The narrator is, in other words, personalized though he is not dramatized, constituting what Genette labels a "narrateur extra-hétérodiégétique."[1] Here, the narrative voice is constantly present as an observer who penetrates the souls of the actors and who unmasks their secrets. Therein, he has a primary role in how history is perceived and received by the reader. He is the one who, endowed with reason, uncovers the "Truth" hidden in history for all concerned. Moreover, he will reveal "l'idée universelle des choses" which transcends the accidents of time and circumstance.

Textual clues that normally announce the exegetic or commentatorial shifter can be, as I have indicated, either present in or absent from the nouvelle. But even when they are absent--that is to say, in those passages that do no contain the linguistic shifter "je"--even in these alleged "objective" passages, the narrator traces his own profile, ensigns his presence.[2]

"The Implicit Shifter"

The introduction of the first nouvelle in *Les Désordres de l'Amour* (the *"avant-récit"*) consists precisely of what could be called objective narration. One can state, for all practical purposes, that there is no commenting voice; the past (referent) is "represented" with seemingly no meaning assigned to it. This is significant as it seems to suggest that the historical events at this point need no clarification, justification, or comment, thereby suggesting also perhaps their relative unimportance for the formulation of the *discours*.[3]

Besides the introduction, which concerns Henri III, and the opening paragraphs of the first part of the nouvelle (which is a continuation of the king's story), there are few such passages in this first nouvelle. These passages are either descriptive, as is the case with the passage describing the château where a part of the action takes place (p. 17); or they allude to some peripheral character, as is the case in that part of the text that concerns the comte de Salmes' visit to the French court which indeed plays no significant role in the events narrated and is mentioned only parenthetically (pp. 20-21). In all of these objective passages, the narration is entirely in the aorist and the events seem to possess the status of the "real" outside of the person of the narrator.

Another sign of the narrator that is a veritable absence of all signs can be found in some of the "scenes" (dialogues and monologues) in the nouvelle that are reported in the direct style without the intrusion of the narrating agent. But whereas the objective passages would seem to signal the relatively secondary nature of the events and situations for the progression of the discursive stance, here, on the contrary, the scenes incorporate what the narrative voice deems most essential. For whereas, in the *roman pré-*

cieux, scenes generally have a very limited
function: "Dans le roman précieux le dialogue
ressemble trop souvent à une discussion de ruelle,
pendant laquelle la vie semble se figer. . .,"[4] in
Mme de Villedieu's nouvelles, by contrast, the
scene has an important dramatic function in
advancing the action. The dialogues in *Les
Désordres de l'Amour*, like those in *La Princesse
de Clèves*, are truly, "theatrical" scenes. All
that is important is *spoken*.

Interestingly, then, there are in this first
story three major scenes (in terms of length) and
nine minor ones. There are in each of the three
major scenes two participants: Mme de Sauve and
the duc de Guise. (As these three dialogues occur
at three of the most critical moments in the development of the plot, even that seventeenth-century
reader expecting to read about the loves of the
king should have had some indication as to the
importance of these two characters.)

The first scene (p. 12) establishes the
relationship between the lovers. From this initial conversation, the reader learns that the duke
is genuinely and totally in love with Mme de Sauve
and that she, on the other hand, is somewhat
indifferent and even slightly uncivil towards him.
But after reporting this scene essentially devoid
of commentary, the narrative voice concludes: "Il
prononçoit ces paroles avec une douleur qui auroit
dû toucher Madame de Sauve. Mais elle se trouvoit
mieux d'un peu de coquetterie que d'un amour si
parfait" (p. 13). Similarly, the second scene
(p. 16) serves to accentuate the extent of his
love and the coldness of her indifference. The
third major scene (p. 38) is the one that reveals
the true tragedy of the situation: it confirms
that the noble and beautiful duc de Guise is, in
the final analysis, weak and totally blinded by
his passion; and that Mme de Sauve, the unworthy
object of his desire, is cruel and immoral.[5]
Moreover, in the remaining nine minor scenes (in
some of which Guise is a participant), it is
always and without exception a question of plots
by Mme de Sauve's enemies to destroy her.

In the two "monologues" of the nouvelle (pp.
49, 60), in the form of letters and devoid of ex-

plicit mediation by the narrating agent, the reader is again exposed to two things: first, to Guise's inability to reason; and, secondly, to the immense tragedy of this potentially great and courageous nobleman destroyed by the ravages of jealousy. If any doubts remain as to who is to occupy center stage in this first nouvelle (the displacement of emphasis away from the king), they are dispelled when one considers its focalizations. The narration here in non-focalized;[6] but by personalizing to a great extent her narrator, Mme de Villedieu, as Francillon has shown to be the case for Mme de Lafayette, avoids many problems of a divine omniscience. First of all, the depth of the vision varies; and, secondly, there is a variation in the point of view.

Most of the characters in the nouvelle (even those that play essential roles in the development of the plot) are the objects of only external and sporadic observations by the narrator. The reader sees them through their attitudes and their words which are merely exposed and rarely analyzed. This is true, for example, for the queen mother who, nonetheless, is an important character in this first story.

Mme de Sauve also is seen only externally; but because of a variation in the point of view she is perceived through several different "optics." The thoughts of Mlle de Châteauneuf as well as those of Mlle d'Elbeuf and the Queen of Navarre, to be more specific, are presented solely when they converse *about* Mme de Sauve; they are represented as personalities only insofar as they influence the destiny of the heroine. Consequently, at times one observes Mme de Sauve "objectively," as in these three scenes, and at other times through the filter of one of the other characters. Thus one sees her (and the action) as Mlle de Châteauneuf sees her: "Cette coquette [une femme] pas de bonne foie, incapable d'un sincere engagement" (p. 19). In a different scene the reader observes with Mlle de Châteauneuf that "c'est une coquette qui ne peut faire la félicité d'un amant délicat. . ." (p. 31); and on a third occasion Mme de Sauve is perceived as "cette enchanteresse" (p. 47). Next, the reader sees the heroine through the eyes of Mlle d'Elbeuf: "De quel charme ou de quel sortilege se sert cette coquette" (p. 25); "Comment cette coquette a-t-elle pu lui [à Guise] faire si tôt oublier. . ." (p. 51).

Finally, in the eyes of her lovers, the King of Navarre, Monsieur, and the duc de Guise, Mme de Sauve appears alternately as "cette coquette," "cette enchanteresse," or "cette belle" depending on whether they are, at the moment in question, blinded by their love or tormented by their jealousy. As a result of this delegation of the point of view, a kind of "indictment" agains Mme de Sauve and her crimes emerges; it is totally convincing because of the corroborative "testimonies." And since in the case of the lovers the particular "Mme de Sauve" that the reader perceives changes abruptly sometimes within the same scene, a composite picture of the heroine "develops" (in the photographic sense) into that of a complex, unseizable personality. One seems never able to pinpoint her essence; she remains a mystery. Significantly, she herself, who is endlessly *spoken of*, speaks the least perhaps of all the characters.

This variation of the point of view is an important aspect of Mme de Villedieu's technique; this psychological relativism, in a manner of speaking, tempers what would otherwise have been the absolute, insistent, excessive point of view of an omniscient narrator if the same effect were to be achieved.[7]

One could now ask what comments and judgments the narrator, in his own name, makes of Mme de Sauve and whether or not they differ from those of the other characters. One finds, however, that the narrating voice appears never to judge explicitly Mme de Sauve; yet, one could almost say that he quite obviously has been influenced by the other characters' appraisals for the narrator too refers to the heroine on several occasions as "cette coquette."[8] In reporting, for example, the final conversation between the lovers, he remarks that

Elle prononçoit ces paroles avec une lang-

ueur si touchante, que le Duc de Guise
en fut ému & qu'aprehendant les suites de
cette émotion, il voulut prendre la fuite,
mais *la dame coquette* le retenant: "Non,
non, lui dit-elle, vous ne m'échaperez pas
. . ." (p. 39, emphasis added)

In the final analysis, the duc de Guise is
the only character that appears to be the object
of a somewhat limited internal analysis through
his "monologues." This appears to be true also in
a few passages where it is a question of the
effect that Mme de Sauve has on him but where the
reader, through the eyes of another character,
penetrates the duke's thoughts and motives before
he himself is aware of them (p. 35).

"The Explicit Exegetic Shifter"

The explicit exegetic shifters in this first
nouvelle are interspersed and integrated into the
prose, often as maxims, and always as reflections
on the "disorders" of passion--whether individual
and personal like jealousy:

Mademoiselle d'Elbeuf avoit elle-même trop
de colere pour s'opposer à celle de la Reine
de Navarre; *la jalousie de la beauté grave
des ressentimens éternels dans le coeur
d'une jeune personne,* & cette princesse ne
reconnoissoit plus le Duc de Guise dans
l'amant de Madame de Sauve. (p.48)

or irrationality, and the loss of willpower:

La personne qui faisoit ce discours devoit
le rendre suspect; *mais l'amour & ses
effets, se reglent rarement par la raison.*
(p. 32)

Il faudroit avoir éprouvé *combien le
dépit des amants est fragile et trompeur,*

> pour bien se presenter l'effet de cet entre-
> tien. (p. 40)
>
> Il ne balança que bien peu sur ce choix; *les
> movements de l'amour sont rapides*; & non
> seulement le Roi de Navarre se determina en
> faveur de sa nouvelle maîtresse, mais il
> entra delicatement dans ses interêts, &
> resolut de faire tomber sur sa rivale, la
> confusion qu'elle lui avoit préparée. (p.
> 23).

or whether these disorders are collective and
national, like civil war:

> . . .il *demeure* pour constant qu'elle [la
> guerre] prit naissance dés l'année 1577 et
> il ne l'*est* pas moins. . .qu'elle eut sa
> source dans les intrigues d'amour. . . (p.
> 65) (all emphasis added)

In each case there is an instantaneous shift from
the aorist to the *present* tense, from the narrative to the discursive mode.

** ** **

Nouvelle II

"The Implicit Shifter"

The implicit exegetic shifter in the second
nouvelle is found almost exclusively in the scenes
since there is relatively little objective narration. There appears to be no mediating voice
especially in the introductory paragraphs of the
first part of this nouvelle. It is here that the
story of the Marquis de Termes is exposed: a

brief history of his lineage, his relationship to Charles IX, and the events leading up to his marriage. Again, the implication here is that the events recounted are clear and require no commentary or elaboration since their position in the articulation of the discursive stance is not primordial. Indeed, as the nouvelle progresses towards its narrative and discursive conclusions, this appears to be true.[9]

If there is little objective narration here, the scene, on the contrary, is what dominates this second nouvelle. The text is, as I have attempted to suggest in Chapter Two, built around two major scenes: the confession and the entrapment.[10] The two scenes constitute the focal points of the two respective parts of the nouvelle because each part is the slow progressive preparation of one of these pivotal scenes of confrontation.

In other words, the nouvelle in its entirety is a series of "incomplete" scenes, or more precisely, it is the same scene repeated and transformed without ever being fully realized. In the first part of the nouvelle the scene is that of a "conversation" between the marquis and the marquise. When the exchange between the spouses finally occurs, this part of the story terminates as the dialogue results in the death of the marquis. In the second part, this pivotal scene is again that of a conversation, this time between the baron de Bellegarde and the former Marquise de Termes, now Mme de Bellegarde; and again, when this conversation is "consummated," the nouvelle ends with the (symbolic) death of her husband.

One can identify no less than eleven major monologues or dialogues (once more, "major" in terms of length and importance) in this nouvelle where the spoken word and subsequently its correlative, the letter, become all powerful. Each scene invariably includes two participants, although one of them may be silent or totally absent. Moreover, it can be noted further that there are three scenes involving M. de Termes and his wife (pp. 70, 72, 76); two between the baron de Bellegarde and his aunt prior to their marriage (pp. 78, 81); and two between Bellegarde and his aunt after she becomes Mme de Bellegarde (pp. 87,

114)--and one of these is essentially a monologue as the baron is speechless. Furthermore, there exist two instances where Bellegarde and his new wife "converse," as it were, through an intermediary; i.e., where her feelings, attitudes, or intentions are made known to him and reciprocally his to her through a third person. In these cases, it is a question of two scenes that occur back to back: first, that of Mme de Bellegarde and the queen mother followed by one between M. de Bellegarde and the queen mother; and, secondly, Amboise de Bussi and Bellegarde followed by a conversation between Amboise de Bussi and Mme de Bellegarde.

It is clear from the beginning that this is not a nouvelle of events but one of words and sentiments. In fact, the story prepares and announces one important historical *event*: the flight of Bellegarde and his subsequent activity in the marquisate of Saluces. It is rather the story of the deterioration of love; it chronicles the effects of this powerful passion upon the private lives and the public functions of its victims.

In the initial scene between the Marquis de Termes and his young wife (p. 70), the reader "sees" (supposedly in an objective and unmediated manner) the deep love and esteem that the marquis holds for his wife. Through his pronouncements to her, one perceives him as honest, sensitive, and genuinely interested in serving as her friend and confidant as well as her husband. By the same token, Mme de Termes is presented "objectively" as tormented and desperate yet concerned not to expose her husband to her terrible secret.

In the second dialogue between the spouses (p. 72), which in reality is a monologue, Mme de Termes' character begins to crystallize. Her confession reveals a weak and defeated woman who would gladly accept her own death as relief from her tormented state. She remains, nevertheless, aware of her own worth and virtue and realizes the extraordinary nature of her confession.

It is during the course of their third and final conversation (p. 76) that the reader observes the Marquis de Termes, in perhaps the true

Cornelian tradition, reconcile his *volonté* and his *passion*; for although he is in love, his ability to reason remains intact. Consequently, in order to insure his wife's *bonheur* he renounces his own. The tragedy here, as in the theater of Corneille, is due to external events ("les astres seuls étoient coupables," p. 74). Indeed, the marquis appears to be a Cornelian hero trapped in a Racinian tragedy.[11] In this same scene, the reader observes, on the part of the marquise, esteem and consideration for her husband dissipate into a selfish and suspicious concern for the "self." The tragedy in her case is not written in the stars but will prove to be a tragedy of choice. On the one hand, she can, out of duty and virtue, choose her husband's *repos* by renouncing her *folle passion*; or, on the other hand, she can assure her own *bonheur* by consummating her love.

In the two conversations between the baron de Bellegarde and the marquise before their nuptials, her speech reveals how passion slowly but methodically might take possession of her soul by effacing all traces of virtue and decency. In the very first of these dialogues (p. 78), her virtue and reason still prove more powerful than her love as it is her duty to the memory of her late husband which seems to dictate her speech. By their second meeting (p. 81), however, passion has begun to take its toll. With her duty to her husband somewhat nullified by the marquis' will, Mme de Termes becomes preoccupied with the consummation of her love and the realization of her future happiness. Yet, when her lover proposes a common-law marriage, she appears still virtuous and reasonable enough to reject it--at least initially.

The first conversation between the Bellegardes as husband and wife suggests, however, that passion has entirely eroded her virtue (p. 87). And her monologue with the queen mother reveals a wife insensitive to her new husband's political disgrace and concerned only with remaining a *maîtresse délicate*:

Il [Bellegarde] m'a fait trouver des dégoûts, poursuivit-elle, dans un mariage qui auroit dû faire toute ma felicité. Il m'a

> fait troubler le repos de l'homme du monde
> qui meritoit le mieux toutes mes affections,
> & aprés m'avoir forcée à renoncer à mes
> parens, à ma patrie, & aux interêts de la
> gloire, c'est encore lui qui me force à
> venir demander à Vôtre Majesté de protéger
> le Marechal de Bellegarde contre lui-même.
> Oui, Madame, la maniere dont il me traite
> lui fait plus de tort que ses plus grands
> ennemis ne lui en sçauroient faire. Tout le
> Piemont, toute la France, & peut-être toute
> l'Europe, car mon avanture est assez extra-
> ordinaire pour y être repanduë, sont témoins
> que, pour cet ingrat, j'ai abandonné ce que
> la gloire & la fortune devoient me rendre
> plus cher. Que peut-on penser de la recom-
> pense que j'en reçois? Il me méprise; il
> m'abandonne; il écrivoit même à la feuë
> Duchesse de Sayoye une lettre qui m'est tom-
> bée entre les mains, par laquelle il la
> suplioit de se porter à des violences contre
> ma personne. . .Si je ne l'aimois encore,
> tout perfide qu'il est, je ne manqueroit pas
> de moyens pour me vanger de tant d'injures.
> (pp. 97-98)

One is presented here with an extremely honest and
lucid character who is able to verbalize the
effects of her passion on her life and reputation.
This lucidity comes too late, however, as it is
only after the fact that the heroine realizes
regretfully that her "passion idiote" has
destroyed her reasoning faculties; it forces her
to forsake not only the memory of a deserving husband and her own *gloire*, it forces her to forsake
her country as well. She is equally lucid enough
to perceive that her husband's love has now modulated from resentment to rancor.

In his own dialogue with the queen mother
(pp. 99-101), M. de Bellegarde's discourse indicates that this beautiful and admirable character
has been reduced to a lying and self-serving con-
spirator. The same is true of his *fausse confidence* to Bussi (p. 104). And the fact that Mme
de Bellegarde is a participant at all in a conversation with Bussi demonstrates the degree to which
she herself has been reduced to a resentful and

spiteful wife still desperately clinging to the only vestiges of virtue that she has left (pp. 109-112, see also Appendix B below).

The final and in fact the only true verbal exchange between these protagonists as husband and wife results from a series of plots and counterplots (p. 114). Their words, now in the form of threats, reveal no trace of the love that previously prompted them to defy the rules of social, political, and religious convention. These utterances indicate, on her part, a remorse for her own predicament and a total indifference toward the object of her once formidable desire; and, on his part, they reveal a loathsome vengeance totally unworthy of a gentlemen of noble birth.

If in most of the other nouvelles of the Classical period dialogue seems to fulfill a limited narrative fuction, in Mme de Villedieu's second nouvelle it advances the action while creating a certain dramatic suspense throughout the text. In this second story, these "spoken" passages constitute small *scènes de théâtre*; for, as in the first nouvelle, the important instances assume the form of speech; each moment of dramatic tension--the confession, the death scene, to name but two--are reported in the direct style.

The narration in Mme de Villedieu's second *Exemple*, as in the first, is non-focalized; here again, however, the depth of the narrator's penetration varies. The feelings and attitudes of the three principal characters alone are scrutinized in addition to being exposed. The other actors, including the queen mother and Bussi who have somewhat important functions, are seen only externally. The reader "knows" them or sees how they react from a distance; they are hardly analyzed. But even for the three protagonists there is a difference in the degree to which they constitute objects of analysis. M. de Termes, for example, (and to a lesser extent, even Bellegarde) is presented principally in his attitude towards his wife, his conversations with her, and in his subsequent actions. He is not therein profoundly analyzed, i.e., "maximized": no general and universal truth or observation serve as commentary on or judgment of his situation.

It is quite clearly Mme de Termes-Bellegarde who is the object of the deepest penetration; but this heroine appears not to be analyzed exclusively by the narrator. As one can see from the analysis above, she is also presented in an objective manner in the scenes of the text which do indeed offer a dramatic way of presenting certain facts with a minimum of narrative intervention. Her conversations offer a kind of change in perspective. For if elsewhere the heroine is the object of a *vision par derrière*, in these instances she appears to be the object of a *vision avec*.[12] This is to say that if in the first instance the reader, through the omniscient narrator, knows the feelings of the heroine and the consequences of her actions *before* she herself is aware of them, then in the latter he follows the evolution of her character and is exposed to her sentiments *as* she herself becomes aware of them. Thus from her initial confession to her first husband to her final confrontation with her second, Mme de Termes-Bellegarde experiences (and the reader follows) the slow, progressive deterioration of a violent passion.

If in the first nouvelle the central character *ne parle guère*, here the heroine *ne fait que parler*; therein lies an essential difference between the two nouvelles. In the first, the mysterious Mme de Sauve is the subject of the conversations of others; she is the *spoken* and rarely the *speaking* subject; her "power" is her physical presence ("la vue de Mme de Sauve"). Mme de Termes-Bellegarde's *force*, on the other hand, is the power of the *verb*; with her words she dominates and silences others and openly speaks about her self, her passion. What the reader learns of her, she *tells* him directly. She is hardly mysterious but appears at times to be all but transparent.

"The Explicit Exegetic Shifter"

The seven explicit exegetic shifters in the

second nouvelle, that is to say, direct interventions by the narrator to comment on or judge the events in question, are also interspersed throughout the prose sometimes in the form of maxims and invariably in the present tense. Here, however, the maxims are not as "obvious" or evident but tend to be more embedded into the past of the *récit* for the reader to extract--(what I shall label as "latent" maxims).

This shifter can function as a kind of footnote to justify what seems an infraction of the rules of *vraisemblance*; when, for example, Mme de Bellegarde is able to intercept (miraculously, it appears) her husband's note to the false marquise by substituting one of her own "laquais" for her husband's messenger, the narrating agent interprose: ". . .elle envoya un des laquis prendre à sa place la réponse qu'il attendoit. Elle portoit mêmes livrées que le Mareschal, & *on ne connoît pas toûjours les laquais par le visage*" [sic] (p. 108).[13] This kind of shifter also functions to justify or to condemn the actions of a character. To explain why the Marquis de Termes chooses not to inform his nephew earlier of Mme de Termes' inclination, the *récit* shifts to *discours* with the following sentence: "Son oncle n'avoit pas eu la force de lui dire ce qu'il sçavoit des sentimens de la marquise; *c'est une nouvelle qu'on ne se resout point à porter soi-même à son rival*. . ." (p. 78). Elsewhere, to explain why after the death of his uncle the young Bellegarde does not challenge the extraordinary provisions of the will, one encounters the following shifter: "Il mourut peu de temps aprés dans les bras de son neveu qui. . .se desesperoit de sa mort, & auroit sans doute combattu de sacrifices & de generosité avec lui, s'il avoit plus longtems vécu. *Mais comme il est inutile, quand les gens ne sont plus, de faire ces suppositions* le baron. . .ne s'y arrêta gueres" (p. 79).

The explicit exegetic shifter in this second nouvelle surfaces usually as a commentary on the devastating effects that love has on reason and as an indirect judgment of a character's weakness. Bellegarde, for example, is subtly condemned for sacrificing his political ambition and *gloire* for physicial pleasure:

> Les premiers jours de ce mariage comblerent
> ces amants de tant de felicité qu'ils en
> étoient comme enivrez; ils ne se regardoient
> & ne se parloient qu'avec transport; un
> moment d'absence leur duroit une année, & *le*
> *Marquis renonçant à tous les desirs qu'une*
> *juste ambition donne aux gens de sa*
> *naissance* sembloit avoir borne sa gloire à
> plaire à sa nouvelle épouse. (p. 85)

In a similar manner, Bussi is judged unfavorably
for becoming the total puppet of his passion: *"Le*
parfait amour rend si docil que d'abord cet amant
consentit à tout ce qu'on souhaitoit. . ." (p.
105).

For the most part, however, these explicit
shifters in the second story are latent maxims
that discourse on the effects of passion on the
heroine herself. In the first instance, one reads
that "La marquise n'étoit pas encore parvenuë au
degré d'amour qui *détruit* entierement la raison"
(p. 82). From this, the following maxim can be
understood: "L'Amour détruit entièrement la
raison." And when Mme de Termes, ignoring convention and *le bon sens*, relinquishes and marries
her nephew, the narrator speculates that" . . .
soit que Bellegarde ne laissât plus aprocher sa
tante que par des gens qui lui parloient en sa
faveur, ou *que ce soit une des fatalitez de*
l'amour d'abuser de la puissance qu'on lui donne,
la marquise se trouva la femme du jeune marquis
. . ." (p. 84). The maxim hidden here ("C'est
une des fatalitez de l'amour d'abuser de la
puissance qu'on lui donne "), an observation of
the marquise's progressive loss of will and
reason, is particularly significant as it is a
paraphrase of the lesson with which the story
begins ("*Qu'on ne peut donner si peu de puissance*
à l'amour qu'il n'en abuse"). And finally, when
Mme de Bellegarde's passion has expired and she is
no longer susceptible to the germs of jealousy,
the narrator inserts a present tense between the
lines of the past: "Madame de Bellegarde n'aimoit
plus assez son mari pour être capable de grande

jalousie. *Il n'y a point d'amour si violent qu'un long mépris ne chasse d'un bon coeur;. . .mais elle étoit naturellement curieuse et se fit un plaisir de rompre à son mari des mesures de galanterie*" (p. 109).

** ** **

Nouvelles III and *IV*

"The Implicit Exegetic Shifter"

The implicit exegetic shifter in the third nouvelle appears frequently as objective narration; for whereas in the other two stories such passages are limited, they constitute a substantial portion of this one. (It is recalled from Chapter One that this is also the most "historical" of the stories). And though the scene still has an important dramatic function, it seems not to appear in precisely the insistent manner as it does in the preceding nouvelle. In the account of Givry's childhood liaison with the Guise family and the commencement of his relation- ship with Mme de Maugiron, the narrator's presence is barely felt. He is equally and conspicuously absent in the narration of the birth of the League and the account of Givry's military courage and strategic position in the royal forces (pp. 120-125).

One can locate three major and five minor scenes in this part of the story. Significantly, in the major scenes, again in dialogic and mono- logic form, one central character (perhaps even the pivotal character), Mlle de Guise, is *absent*. Much like Mme de Sauve in the first nouvelle, this princess is the *spoken* and rarely the *speaking* subject. In the first of these three dialogues (pp. 129-130), not only is Mlle de Guise a non- participant but her identity has not yet been established, though it is she and her poetry that (in a sense) "motivate" the conversation. It is here that one sees the effect of the mysterious verses on Givry and especially on his attitude towards Mme de Maugiron. Yet what seems essential in this scene is the documentation of the intimate and seemingly eternal bond of friendship between Givry and Bellegarde; for they, in the final analysis, are perhaps the principal actors whose lives and destinies will furnish further examples of the disorders of love. For whereas in the other nouvelles it is the lover (husband)/mistress scene that comprises the nucleus of the story, here, on the contrary (and though this scene proves still to be an important one), it is the confrontation between the two male rivals--a scene that is totally absent or merely suggested in the preceding stories--upon which the plot hinges.

In spite of the previous "objective" description of Givry as the epitome of perfection in both mind and body, already in this initial dialogue one finds evidence that even he could be debilitated by this disease called passion. One observes how his genuine and heretofore faithful love and respect for one of the world's most honest and attractive women becomes infected with the microbes of self-interest and pride:

> J'avouë, poursuivit Givry, que je suis amoureux de Madame de Maugiron, & que je ne renoncerois pas à cette passion pour des vers dont j'ignore le dessein, mais si Mademoiselle de Guise les avoit considerez comme une faveur, Madame de Maugiron ne m'empêcheroit pas d'y être sensible. Je suis jeune, j'ai de l'ambition, & Mademoiselle de Guise est une des plus belles princesses du monde. On me traiteroit d'insensé si, pouvant avoir une intrigue d'amour avec elle, j'en manquois l'occasion. (p. 131)

In the second of these scenes (the longest of the entire nouvelle), Mlle de Guise is still a non-participant while her presence continues to be felt through her verses, these "traces" of her talent ("essai de ses talents"). This is the dialogue between the hero and the baron de Vins (p. 133), an attaché of the Guise party who has been taken prisoner. It sets the stage for the subsequent conflict between the hero's duty to the king and the affairs of state on the one hand and his desire to satisfy his own concupiscence on the other. At this particular point he articulates quite effectively the reasons for his devotion to the king which, for the moment at least, is the *ressort* of his existence: "Je suis né sujet du Roi que je sers, & avant que je fusse en âge de faire un choix, on m'avoit inspiré une soûmission aveugle pour les lois de cette obeïssance" (p. 133). The baron de Vins has only to evoke the image of the princess, however, for this devotion to the monarch to assume the status of a subordinate influence or catalyst in the hero's life. In fact, duty to both His Majesty and his mistress diminishes; and "par une fatalité qu'il ne pouvoit éviter, il révoit malgré lui incessamment à Mademoiselle de Guise, & ne songeoit plus qu'à peine à Madame de Maugiron" (p. 137).

The third major scene (p. 169) is in reality a monologue. Givry's confession to the king reveals the extent to which this passion has eroded his courage and character. Rejected by the object of his desire, he is now wounded, weak, and despondent. In addition, his ability to reason has been impaired as he is now totally and irreparably obsessed with his passion:

> Givry fut dangereusement blessé à l'épaule & la tristesse dont il étoit possedé augmentant le peril où le mettoit sa blessure, les chirurgiens le jugerent à l'extremité de sa vie. . .il haïssoit la vie, &. . .il étoit bien aise de se voir en danger de la perdre. Il raconta [au roi] ce qui étoit arrivé à Corbeil, & ce recit lui ayant causé des émotions qui lui firent croire qu'il étoit prêt d'expirer. (p. 168)

Moreover, in the minor scenes of the story, attention is invariably channelled towards two important factors: the deterioration of the hero's consideration for Mme de Maugiron, a change that is both irrational and heedless; and his progressive destruction by passion. In one such scene (with Mme de Maugiron, p. 139), Givry resorts to lies and half-truths to explain his disinterest in his mistress. In another (p. 145), one sees the hero consciously and deliberately ignore his duty as a military officer and as a subject of the king when he permits a shipment of provisions to reach Paris--a costly gesture dictated exclusively by his new master, love.

It is perhaps significant that in the single scene where Mlle de Guise is bodily present, she is still absent in another respect insofar as she pretends not to recognize Givry and *speaks* to him as if he were a stranger:

> Mademoiselle de Guise avoit parfaitement conservé l'idée de Givry, & le reconnut dés le premier mot qu'il prononca. Mais elle voulut se divertir de cette rencontre. . . [en le] traitant comme un avanturier inconnu. (p. 152)

She is absent in still another way in that, even after she is forced to recognize Givry, he can neither declare his love nor demand an explanation for the verses.

It is only in the fourth nouvelle (the continuation of Givry's story) that Mlle de Guise appears truly as both the speaking and the spoken subject. This last nouvelle pulsates on a series of parallel scenes which include, first, Givry and the princess and, secondly, Givry and Bellegarde. Each instance turns out to be invariably a scene *about* the letter written in the hero's name. Each interview with the loved one follows or precedes a confrontation with the rival; and it is the repetition and the alternation of these scenes that constitute the nouvelle proper. As Givry's desire for Mlle de Guise intensifies, respect and consideration for Bellegarde diminishes until his ultimate rejection by the first provokes finally a physical assault on the second.

The constant reprise and the persistent pulsation of these two scenes are punctuated by two others: that between Givry and his neglected mistress and that between Givry and the king. The

first reveals the magnitude of the hero's
malhonnêteté; the second, the depth of his
désespoir. The story attains its climax when the
two suitors confront each other for the final
time. Significantly, it is the only such confrontation in the fourth nouvelle where the *enjeu*
itself, the princess, is also present (pp.
195-198).

Mme de Villedieu's *exemples* are con-
sistently non-focalized; and this one is no exception. But again, as in the other stories, the
depth of the vision varies. In the two final
nouvelles only two of the characters are presented
with any degree of profundity: Givry and Mme de
Maugiron. One would expect perhaps that Mlle de
Guise, as the one character who motivates the
narration, would be one of those analyzed. But in
the manner of Mme de Sauve of the first nouvelle,
the princess remains to a large extent mysterious
and is unquestionably the most *talked about*
character. And, as I have suggested, it is principally those characters of Mme de Villedieu that
verbalize their interiority who are analyzed--or,
more precisely, who analyze themselves since the
narrator rarely engages in the omniscient and
direct penetration of a character. Rather, they
are put on stage; they speak their characters and
personalities, engage in introspection.

In this respect, both Mlle de Guise and
Bellegarde are presented only externally.
Bellegarde indeed does speak; but his observations
and perceptions are articulated for and about his
friend Givry and never himself. Apropos of the
princess, a contradicton exists between what is
said of her by the other protagonists (especially
by Givry) and the image that emerges when she herself speaks: in the latter rare instance she
appears as capricious, self-serving, and arrogant.
The reader feels no sympathy for either the princess or Bellegarde.

The tragedy of the story surfaces in the
fate of Givry and especially in that of Mme de
Maugiron. Her character crystallizes during the
dialogue with her inconstant lover; and though she
remains unrealistically hopeful and blindly
devoted to Givry, she is, nevertheless, extraor-

dinarily lucid as to the nature and the extent of her own *manie*:

> Vous reviendrez quelque jour à moi, lui disoit-elle & il est impossible que tant de constance ne touchent enfin vôtre coeur. . .
>
> Ne vous repaissez point de cette chimere, repliquoit Givry. . .s'il faut vous avoüer toutes mes indifferences, je pense que j'aimerois plutôt une troisiéme personne, que je ne retournerois à vous.
>
> Pousse tes duretez plus loin, reprit Madame de Maugiron, en versant quelques larmes, & ajoute que tu me hais plus que tu ne m'as aimée! Je ne t'en aimerai pas moins pour cela; ma fatale passion n'a besoin d'aucun espoir pour subsister, & il y a long-tems que sans lui elle semble reprendre de nouvelles forces. Tu ne m'en dois aucune reconnoissance, ce n'est pas un amour volontaire; mais tu me dois quelque pitié de ce que les astres me traitent avec tant de rigueur.

(pp. 190-191)

In a comparable manner, Givry himself is hopelessly and unrealistically in love with the indifferent and illusive Mlle de Guise; yet he too, in his confessions to the king and in his excuses to Mme de Maugiron, proves to be extremely perceptive and adept in self-analysis:

> Mais, Madame, [lui dit-il] je suis un miserable qui ne puis joüir des faveurs du sort, & qui malgré le blâme secret que je donne à mon coeur, ne puis le guérir de son relâchement. Ayez-en le mépris qu'il merite, Madame, & sans porter vos bontez jusques à venir me reprocher mon inconstance, abandonnez-moi à mes dissipations & mes tiedeurs. . .j'aime Mademoiselle de Guise jusques à la fureur, & je suis capable des derniers effets du desespoir si

109

je la vois me préferer un rival de ma qualité. Peut-être que sans murmure je la
verrois épouser un grand prince; mais je ne
puis sans mourir lui voir de la complaisance
pour les feux d'un homme de mon rang.

(pp. 185-187)

"The Explicit Exegetic Shifter"

There is a slight reduction in the
occurrence of the explicit exegetic shifter in the
last two nouvelles. In the third, one can locate
six such shifters which are in the present tense
and integrated (as maxims) into the aorist of the
story. It is perhaps not without significance
that they apply specifically to Givry. Each one
marks an intervention by the narrating agent to
comment, to analyze, or to judge the progression
of the hero's malady.

To explain why he becomes so easily infatuated with the mere thought that a beautiful
princess might be regarding him favorably--an
infatuation that on the surface seems to contradict the image of the wise and honest Givry that
has just been evoked--the *récit historique* modulates gracefully into the discursive mode: "Givry
avoit fort admiré Mademoiselle de Guise quand elle
étoit enfant. Il consideroit en lui-même le degré
de charmes où elle devoit être parvenüe, & *c'est
une douce tentation pour un homme de vingt & un
ans, que les avances de galanterie d'une belle &
grande princessse*" (p. 130).

Or, to justify why initially the otherwise
lucid Givry, "qui avoit reçu des faveurs de la
nature qui l'affranchissoiént de la regle des
tems" (p. 122), seems completely irrational and
more or less unconscious at this point of his own
true feelings, the narrator intrudes:

Givry n'étoit pas encore bien persuadé que
Mme de Maugiron dît vrai. *L'amour se*

110

déguise dans ses commencemens, & bien qu'on
pût appeller de ce nom ce qu'il sentoit pour
Mademoiselle de Guise, il n'en étoit pas
tombé d'accord avec lui-même. (p. 139)

And to explain the hero's miraculous reco-
very after the counterproductive gesture on the
part of his friend Bellegarde, the discursive
string again interfuses with the narrative fabric:

Il n'avoit point écrit à Mademoiselle de
Guise. . .il ne sçavoit s'il devoit
s'affliger, ou se réjoüir, de ce qu'on avoit
ainsi declaré son secret, & comme, toutes
choses bien considerées, *il est toûjours
plus avantageux qu'un amant soit connu pour
ce qu'il est que de voir ses feux ignorez,*
il repirt un peu de courage, & cette
dispostion d'esprit jointe à la bonté de son
temperament, commencerent à dissiper les
frayeurs qu'on avoit pour sa vie. (p. 170)

There are three other occasions in this
third *exemple* where the present of the representation pervades into the past of the event. In
the first instance, the historical *énoncé* "il fut
surpris de cette ré-ponse" (it is a question of
Givry's reaction to Mlle de Guise's rejection of
his gifts) is modalized by *"on peut juger combien
. . . "* The result is that attention is drawn to
the utterance which receives a force and an intensity that would have been impossible had the verb
simply been modified adverbially, retaining the
statement at the level of *récit*.[14] In the second
and third instances, the discursive intervention
embeds itself so symmetrically into the historical
utterance that it passes almost unnoticed. The
second concerns the consequences of Givry's very
unprofessional gesture with the shipment of grain:
"[Cette action] fut rapportée au Roi, & *comme le
merite va rarement sans envieux,* on y donna les
plus mauvaises couleurs qu'elle pouvoit recevoir"
(p. 145); the third concerns the hero's attitude
towards his mistress: ". . .il conservoit pour
elle une de ces passions d'habitude, qui sans
avoir l'ardeur d'un commencement d'amour, ne

laissent pas de disputer le terrain à la pleine tranquillité" (p. 156). In each case, it serves as a kind of footnote to situate or to explicate the event.

There are even fewer explicit exegetic shifters in the fourth nouvelle. As in the very first story, they appear here uniquely as maxims on the disorders of love. Apropos of Mlle de Guise, it is a question of the *caprice* of this passion:

> *L'amour est tout plein de caprices, & on ne peut en imaginer de si extravagans dont il ne soit capable.* Mademoiselle de Guise avoit été veritablement irritée de la temerité dont elle accusoit Givry, & ce qui lui déplaisoit en lui devoit lui déplaire dans tous les gentilshommes du royaume. Il n'y en avoit aucun mieux fait, & plus en passe d'une grande élevation que Givry: Mademoiselle de Guise avoit même un fond d'estime & de tendresse pour lui. *Cependent, par une manie dont on ne voit des exemples que dans l'amour,* elle trouva singuliere l'action du Grand Ecuyer [Bellegarde], & sentit une curiosité extraordinaire pour en sçavoir le motif. (p. 177)

And Mme de Maugiron, of course, appears as one of the supreme examples of the *extravagance* of love:

> . . .il n'y a rien que [Givry] n'eût voulu faire pour voir cette femme dégagée, *mais on ne guerit pas de ce mal aussi aisément qu'on en devient malade.* Elle continua à l'aimer malgré lui, & malgré elle, et il retourna à Melun aussi injuste et aussi ingrat qu'elle l'avoit trouvé an arrivant à Gisors. (p. 191)

But whereas in the previous nouvelles such maxims integrated into the prose appear uniquely as instances where *récit* shifts into *discours*, that is to say, explicit moral "intermezzos" by the narrator, in this final one these aphorisms appear also as utterances or as pronouncements from the mouths of the characters themselves. When attempting to account for the expiration of his once ardent and seemingly steadfast passion for Mme de Maugiron, for example, Givry *himself* writes this explanation: ". . .qu'il auroit voulu pouvoir l'aimer toute sa vie; mais qu'*on n'étoit point le maître des mouvemens de son coeur. . .*" (p. 166). Again, when attempting to persuade his former mistress that he can be held accountable neither for his inconstancy nor for his irrationality, he contends: "Mais, Madame, *on n'aime point par choix: et les caprices du coeur sont les tirans de la raison* (p. 187). And during their last interview, Givry says the following:

> Je conviens que vous meritez un coeur plus fidelle, & que je suis injuste quand je répons si mal à vôtre tendresse; mais *en fait d'amour, le discernement de la raison n'opere rien sur le coeur...*(p. 190)

In a similar manner and on a different occasion, it is the king who is the source of the moral wisdom and psychological observation: "*Les caprices d'une jeune personne dont le coeur n'est encore determiné à rien*, repartit le Roi , *sont aussi changeans que vastes*" (p. 194).

This seems to confirm my contention in the preceding chapter that in the final story the moral dilemma is articulated in terms of a certain immediacy which posits and valorizes the present and whereby the characters themselves, acting as autonomous subjects, become capable of discoursing on the malfeasance of love.[15] The presentation of the protagonists as commentators on human imperfections therefore parallels the movement from the poetic maxim of the narrator to the poetry of the heroine that delineates this final story.

Nouvelle I

Logistic shifters integrated into the prose can also be either implicit or explicit. I shall consider the explicit ones because of the peculiar problems that they pose for the text as a whole.[16] During the course of the narrative (*récit*), these shifters act as indicators of the internal organization of the discourse (*discours*). They could assume several forms but seem to have principally a deictic (locative/temporal) function.

They might specify, as in the first nouvelle for example, what the narrative is about as far as the time of the event and the participants discussed: "Ce prince. . .qui jouë un si grand personnage *dans le siecle que je traite*" (p. 5). Therefore, one sees this kind of shifter when, after the introduction of a new character, the narrator pauses briefly to explain who this character is and his relation to the events in question. This occurs, for example, when Dugua, who plays a very minor role in this first story, is initially introduced: "Il *faut* savoir à qui cette fause confidence étoit addressée: Dugua. . ." (p. 46). More often, however, this type of shifter occurs to announce the contents of a particular section of the text as when, for instance, it is a question of the duc de Guise's letter to Mme de Sauve: ". . .une lettre dont *j'ai crû* qu'on seroit bien aise de voir *ici* une copie" (p. 49).

In a similar manner, the logistic shifter sometimes indicates the limits of the narrative, things that will not be represented or narrated usually because of the limits of the "art" of narrating itself. When evoking, for instance, the duc de Guise's ecstasy when he feels assured of his mistress' affections, the narrator explains almost apologetically: ". . .il se laissa transporter à des mouvements de joïe qu'*on trahit* quand *on entreprend* de les dépeindre par des paroles" (p. 40). Or, once again, when attempting to

114

describe the duke's happiness, the narrator again admits his inability to do so: "On ne *peut* pas dire combien le duc de Guise eut de joïe de ce changement" (p. 42).

There are, as well, shifters that indicate the narrator's source, cited frequently in order to justify the position or attitude expounded: ". . .*l'histoire dit* que cet amour étoit encore le motif de son [le comte de Salmes] voyage" (p. 20). And as conclusive proof that the civil war that divided France had its origins in the court disorders, the narrator declares:

> . . .il demeure constant qu'elle [la guerre] prit naissance dés l'année 1577 et il ne l'est pas moins, comme *les Mémoires* sur lesquels *je fais* ce commentaire en font foi, qu'elle eut sa source dans les intrigues d'amour que *je viens* d'écrire. (p. 65)

This brings to surface perhaps the most important, or at least the most conspicuous, logistic shifters in this first story: the ones that recall, underline, and reinforce what has already been presented. They are important as they constitute definite clues as to the orientation of the *discours vis à vis* the *récit*. In the first part of the nouvelle, numerous historical characters are catalogued and the narrator has to recall and rename the ones who will be the focus of the present narration: "il fut tel qu'il fit apprehender pour [la vie du Roi], ou pour sa raison; *les dames dont j'ai déja parlé* redoublerent leurs efforts pour le soulager, & cet honneur sembla reservé à Mademoiselle d'Elbeuf; mais enfin le Roi se determina en faveur de Madame de Sauve" (p. 9). Much in the same way, the reader is reminded of the importance of Guise's letter to Mme de Sauve: ". . .mais la *lettre que je viens de* raporter lui faisant trouver licite tout ce qui servoit à sa vengeance, il envoya conferer avec le prince. . ." (p. 52). To recall a fact alluded to earlier in the story but that the reader may have forgotten, the narrator recalls that "*j'ai dit dans un autre endroit de cette histoire* que le Prince de Condé étoit chef des Protestants d'Allemagne" (p. 51).

It is this kind of shifter that dominates
the third and final part of the first nouvelle:
that part of the text which is almost entirely
meta-narrative in nature. This is to say that it
defines the *project* of the narrator. Each paragraph here is either retrospective, as when the
narrating agent summarizes the essential elements
of the nouvelle and assesses the success of his
undertaking:

> Par cette fatale passion, le Roi de Navarre
> & le Duc de Guise se diviserent; par elle,
> Monsieur se sentit porté à s'allier avec les
> étrangers & donna le funeste exemple de les
> introduire dans le coeur de la France; les
> désordres domestiques de la Maison royale,
> ceux qui troublerent le mariage du Roi de
> Navarre & de la Reine sa femme, les mécon-
> tentemens du Duc de Guise, & l'extremité où
> ils le porterent; *tout cela, dis-je a sa*
> *principale cause dans l'amour. Il n'est que*
> *trop suffisament prouvé par les diverse*
> *intrigues qui composent cet exemple*, que
> l'amour est le ressort de toutes les
> passions de l'ame, & que si on examinoit
> soigneusement les motifs secrets des revolu-
> tions qui arrivent dans les monarchies, on
> le trouveroit toûjours coupable ou complice
> de toutes. (pp. 65-66)

or it is prospective in nature, as when the narrator announces what is to follow in a subsequent
exemple and the relationship (both narrative and
discursive) of this second nouvelle to the one
just presented:

> Je vais tâcher à prouver de même que s'il
> [l'amour] est funeste dans ses excez, il
> n'est pas moins à redouter dans ses
> commencemens; l'histoire du Maréchal de
> Bellegarde & de la Marquise de Termes
> s'offre à propos à ma mémoire pour fournir
> cette seconde preuve.
>
> Ils étoient contemporains des personnes que
> j'ai déja citées, & comme à remonter jusqu'à
> la source des troubles, on trouve qu'ils

auroient été évitez si le Roi Henri III
avoit voulu à son avenement à la couronne
donner la paix generale au Royaume, non
seulement l'histoire du Maréchal de
Bellegarde est une leçon fameuse des soins
qu'on doit prendre pour combattre les pre-
mieres impressions de l'amour, mais elle me
sert à joindre aux galanteries de mon sujet
les veritez importantes de l'histoire
generale. (p. 66)

** ** **

Nouvelle II

The logistic shifter appears and functions
in the second nouvelle much as it does in the
first. These parts of the text that refer to the
code and the encoder, in a manner of speaking, are
characterized by the first person pronoun and the
present, perfect, or future tenses. These "intra-
narrative" positions (in the sense that they
constitute positions in the narrative that refer
to other positions in this *same* narrative) are
used in the first instance to identify and to
clarify the role of one of the protagonists:
"Alors elle lui raconta comme dés son enfance,
elle avoit eu une violent inclination pour *ce même
Baron de Bellegarde dont j'ai parlé. . .*" (p.72)
In the second instance it alerts the reader (or
decoder) as to a change in the code thereby
simplifying the decoding process: ". . .le baron
[de Bellegarde], *que nous appellerons à l'avenir*
le Marquis de Bellegarde, ne s'y arrêta gueres"
(p. 79).

This shifter can also be "inter-narrative";
that is to say, it can refer to the activity of
the narrator, not in the production of the present
narrative, but in the preceding one. When
Damville and Bussi, who are characters in the
first nouvelle, are re-introduced here, one reads:

> Le Duc Damville qui, *comme je l'ai dit dans
> l'histoire precedente*, étoit chef des
> rebelles de Languedoc. . . (p. 90)

> Deux ou trois des plus honnêtes gens de la
> suite du Roi lui [à Mme de Bellegarde]
> firent un hommage de leur desirs &
> entr'autres *Bussi d'Amboise*, favori de
> Monsieur, *dont j'ai déja dit* un mot dans la
> premiere partie. (p. 101)

Or when there is a parenthetical reference to the
queen mother's opposition to Henri III's affair
with the princesse de Condé (which is mentioned
in the first story), the narrator indicates that
"*j'ai dit ailleurs* l'intérêt que la Reine avoit de
s'oposer à ce mariage, & les obstacles qu'elle
tâchoit d'y apporter" (p. 97). It is also with
this statment (shifter) that the narrator links
the first and second nouvelles, at least narratively if not yet discursively.

The entire final paragraph of the second
nouvelle, as a logistic shifter, is retrospective
and prospective and is both intra- and inter-
narrative. Here the narrator summarizes and
underscores what has taken place in both the first
and second *exemples* thereby conjoining the two,
this time discursively as well as narratively:

> Ainsi ce même amour qui dans la premiere
> partie de cet ouvrage a produit les semences
> de la Ligue, met dans celle-ci un obstacle
> secret à la paix generale du royaume, & nous
> a couté une étendue de terre qui ne pourroit
> être reconquise qu'au prix de beaucoup de
> sang & de beaucoup de travaux. (p. 117)

At this point the narrator completely leaves the
narrative mode and enters the domain of discourse
as he assesses the success and the outcome of his
present and past projects:

. . .par les deux exemples qui fournissent
ce premier & second tome, j' ai à ce que
je pense, suffisamment prouvé que l'amour
est le ressort de toutes les autres passions
de l'ame, & qu'on ne peut le combattre trop
tôt, puisque ses moindres étincelles pro-
duisent de funestes embrasemens. (p. 118)

Although the restating of the lessons of the
first and second nouvelles at this point seems to
fuse and conclude these two stories with a degree
of finality ("C'est assez dire, ce me semble, qu'
on ne peut trop en employer pour se garantir d'une
si funeste passion", p. 117), this final paragraph
is also prospective for it announces what is to
follow in a subsequent *exemple* and establishes the
rapport of this forthcoming story with the preceding ones--its rapport in the domain of *récit:*

Mais comme les partisans secrets qu'elle
[la passion] a dans nôtre ame ne peuvent
être vaincus que par un grand nombre de com-
bats, il faut leur opposer divers exemples,
& aprés avoir découvert la source de la
Ligue, tracer un fidele tableau de ses
horreurs & de ses homicides, je la prendrai
dans le commencement de sa declaration, & la
conduirai jusques au siège de Laon, qui fut
pour ainsi dire son agonie. (p. 117)

and its rapport as *discours:*

Dans ces cinq ou six années de son cours, il
ne s'est rien fait de memorable où l'amour
n'ait autant de part qu'il en eut à son origine. . .j'espere ne rapporter pas de moindres preuves, que non seulement il fait agir
nos passions, mais qu'il merite souvent tout
le blâme que ses passions peuvent attirer;
qu'il nous conduit jusques au desespoir, &
que les plus parfaits ouvrages de la nature
et de l'art dependent quelquefois d'un
moment de son caprice & de ses fureurs.[17]

(p. 118)

In the third and fourth nouvelles, the logistic shifter rarely charts intra-narrative stances but rather inter-narrative ones written in the perfect or future tenses and serving, for example, to specify the principal actors in the event: ". . . *le même* Duc de Guise dont *j'ai parlé* dans le premier de *mes* exemples" (p. 119); "Le Marquis de Bellegarde, Grand Ecuyer de France, & neveu de celui dont *j'ai fait* l'histoire dans *la partie precedente*" (p. 128). It also outlines what will (or will not) be included in the narrative as, for example, in this description of Givry: "Il possedoit les langues grecque, latine, & toutes les langues vivantes de l'Europe. . .& *je marquerai* dans la suite de cette histoire, qu'à vingt-deux ans il fut mis à la tête de la cavalerie legere de France" (pp. 122-123).

And, as in the first nouvelle, the logistic shifter marks the present-tense intervention of the narrator when he feels obligated to justify his position by documenting his source. As a justification for such an insistent description and the subsequent valorization of the siege of Rouen as well as the narrator's contention that it was during this particular battle (as oppposed to some possible other) that Givry was nearly mortally wounded, one reades that *"l'histoire fait mention de ce siège* comme l'un des plus chauds qui ait été fait pendant toutes ces guerres" (p. 167). Moreover, to render *vraisemblable* and legitimate his claim that he has consulted the original copy of Givry's death letter to Mlle de Guise, the narrator is again compelled to justify this claim: "Cette lettre ne fut point rendue à Mademoiselle de Guise, l'homme qui la lui aportoit fut fait prisonnier par un parti ennemi, & *c'est sans doute pourquoi elle est parvenue jusques à nous"* (p. 206).

The final paragraph of the fourth nouvelle, as a shifter of logistics, constitutes a succinct summary of all the historical events of the three stories. Furthermore, this passage concludes the entire work and assures it a definite unity:

Les exemples que j'ai choisis pour persuader
la malignité de l'amour ne pouvoient finir
par une histoire plus capable d'inspirer
tout l'horreur qu'il merite. . .

Ainsi finissent presque toutes les personnes
qui s'abandonnent sans reserve à cette
fatale manie. Si on la ressent foiblement,
elle est une source intarissable de perfidie
& d'ingratitude [*one has only to recall the
story of Mme de Sauve and the duc de Guise*];
& si on s'y soûmet de bonne foi, elle mene
jusques à l'exces du déreglement [*as history
substantiates in the case of Mme de Termes-
Bellegarde*] & du desespoir [*as one has just
read in the biographies of Mme de Maugiron
and Givry*]. (p. 208-209)

This constitutes, however, a discursive
rather a strictly narrative coherence; for no
historical (that is to say, chronological) unity
exists necessarily between the stories as they are
presented in Mme de Villedieu's text. They are
detached from the historical continuum; and taken
together, they hardly represent an unbroken horizontal chain. Yet this syntagmatic concatenation
is replaced or superseded by a paradigmatic
"collinearity" through which each of these independent stories assumes its particular position
and by which the ensemble receives it signification.[18]

** ** **

What are, in the final analysis, the consequences of these "traces" of the *énonciation* in
the *énoncé*? Does the "friction" of these two
instances or moments--the moment of the event, the
moment of its evocation--produce any immediately
noticeable results? It is evident that that which
constitutes the *discours* in Mme de Villedieu's
text fragments the linearity of the historical
récit. It is equally evident that the linearity

121

of the *discours* itself is denied: i.e., if the *discours* is interspersed at strategic points throughout the unfolding of the historical narrative, then, in the process, it must bring about its own fragmentation. As the discursive elements fragment the *récit*, however, they simultaneously add to it a kind of vertical depth.

Indeed, in this Classical text neither history nor the discourse on history is linear; rather, the two assume the dimensions of an equation or metaphor in relation to each other. As a result, there is a kind of "dialogue" between the *récit historique* and the narrator's *discours* that postulates a new logic or a different meaning for the past events. This "dialogïzing" is how the *nouvelle historique* is born and it should, therefore, lead to some definitive observations about the form of *Les Désordres de l'Amour* in particular and to some preambulary observations about the nature of this kind of Classical genre in general. Hence, it will be towards these kinds of considerations that I shall direct my attention in the final chapters of this study.

NOTES

CHAPTER THREE

1. Genette, *Figures III*, p. 256.

2. See note 4 of Chapter Two, p. 82.

3. This first nouvelle begins in this manner:

> Les glorieux commencemens du regne de Henri III promettoient des suites semblables. C'estoit un prince charmant par sa personne, qui avant dix-huit ans avoit gagné deux batailles, & qui par un apprentissage de royauté devoit sçavoir l'art de gouverner sagement un peuple.
>
> Il étoit impatiemment attendu sur ces esperances, & les regrets que formoit la Pologne pour sa perte rendoient la joïe des François plus parfaite. La Reine sa mère fut devant de lui jusques aux frontières de l'Estat de Savoie, elle lui presenta le Duc d'Alençon son frère, qu'on appelloit alors Monsieur, & le Roi de Navarre son beau-frère, qui pendant son absence avoient attenté quelque chose contre son autorité & qui pour cela avoient été retenus prisonniers. Il leur pardonna généreusement cette faute; il ne parloit que de rétablir l'abondance & la tranquillité dans le royaume, de prendre une connoissance parfaite de ses affaires, & d'y donner tous ses soins. (pp. 3-5)

4. Roger Francillon, *L'Oeuvre Romanesque de Madame de La Fayette*, p. 218.

5. At the conclusion of this scene, it is explained that:

> Bien que ces paroles du Duc de Guise fussent aussi dures que les precedentes, le ton en

étoit different, & Madame de Sauve étoit
trop sçavante sur ces distinctions pour ne
pas s'en appercevoir. Elle soûpira, elle
laissa couler quelques larmes de dépit, qu'
elle fit passer pour des larmes d'amour, &
joignant à ces pleurs simulez des serremens
de main, & des regards que le coeur du duc
ne pouvoit encore méconnoître, elle lui fit
si bien oublier toutes ses resolutions, qu'
avant qu'ils se separassent, ils prirent
heure pour achever le lendemain leur expli-
cation. (p. 40)

6. What Genette calls *"focalisation zéro"*
(*Figures III*, p. 206).

7. In his analysis of *La Princesse de Clèves*,
Francillon exposes a somewhat comparable technique
on the part of Mme de Lafayette.

8. Examples to be found in passages on the
following pages: 24, 39, 58, 59.

9. This is equally true in the second part of
this story in the account of the initial days of
bliss of the Bellegarde marriage and in the
account of the baron's disgrace and subsequent
ingratiation with Henri III after after Charles
IX's death:

Les premiers jours de ce mariage comblerent
ces amans de tant de felicité, qu'ils en
étoient comme ennivrez; ils ne se parloient
qu'avec transport; un moment d'absence leur
duroit une année, & le marquis. . .sembloit
avoir borné sa gloire à plaire à sa nouvelle
épouse. (p. 85)

10. See, for example, pp. 62-69 of this study.

11. M. de Termes seems to possess some of the
qualities and perhaps the potential of a Cornelian
hero: i.e., "une âme généreuse, un être bien né
doué d'une volonté à côté de la raison, la
magnanimité," etc.; for, somewhat like Rodrigue
(*Le Cid*), he seems endowed with a 'perfect love'

which above all else is one capable of sacrificing its own satisfaction. Just prior to his death, the marquis again displays this *générosité*; for in spite of his wife's confession he continues to love her to the point even of renouncing all of his worldly possessions and his own happiness to guarantee hers.

But the atmosphere of the court and the other characters that surround M. de Termes suggest rather the components of a Racinian tragedy. For whereas the moral perfection of a généreux (which results from the harmonization of *désir* and *liberté*) is possible precisely because desire is directed only towards worthy objects, Mme de Termes hardly constitutes a worthy object. For the marquise as well as for Bellegarde, love is vindictive and possessing; instead of exalting the character, it destroys him (see, e.g., Paul Bénichou, *Les Morales du Grand Siècle*).

12. I borrow these two terms, *vision par derrière* and *vision avec*, from J. Pouillon, *Temps et Roman* (Paris: Gallimard, 1946) and from Francillon, *l'Oeuvre Romanesque de Madame de Lafayette*.

13. As with all the citations in this chapter, including those concerning the logistic shifter in the next section, all emphasis has been added.

14. The statment would remain semantically the same were it written: "Il fut *très* surpris de cette ré-ponse."

Another example is found in the fourth nouvelle where it is a question of Mlle de Guise's reaction to Bellegarde's letter and where the historical statement ("la rareté de l'avanture la lui faisoit envisager avec des yeux plus humains que ceux dont la premiere fois elle avoit lu cette lettre") is modalized by "*il est certain que. . .*"

15. See Chapter Two above.

16. These problems will be discussed in more detail in the concluding chapters of this study. As for the *implicit logistic* shifter, I could study (as Genette does for Proust in *Figures III*) the temporal order, frequency, and duration of the

"histoire" (story) as opposed to the temporal order, frequency, and duration of the "récit" (narration). However, this kind of analysis would constitute only a digression in light of the type of study that I am proposing here.

17. It is here for the first time that the reader is addressed directly and where the discourse of the *narrataire* (the "tu") is incorporated explicitly in the text:

> Je ne doute point qu'en cet endroit plus d'un lecteur ne dise d'un ton irronique que je n'en ai pas toujours parlé de cette sorte, mais c'est sur cela même que je me fond pour en dire tant de mal, & c'est pour en avoir fait une parfaite experience que je me trouve autorisée à le peindre avec de si noires couleurs. (p. 118)

18. The fact that Mme de Villedieu has arranged the events of history in a paradigmatic perspective will be discussed further in Part III of this analysis.

PART III

THE NOUVELLE HISTORIQUE

(SIGNIFICATION)

CHAPTER FOUR

HISTOIRE AND THE *NOUVELLE HISTORIQUE*:

THE *"METAPHORIZATION"* OF HISTORY

Classified as a *nouvelle historique*, *Les Désordres de l'Amour* belongs to a genre that distinguishes itself both by its methods and by its materials. The "marriage" of history and fiction appears to be suggested even in Montaigne.[1] And from this suggestion François de Grenaille, around 1642, composed *Les Amours Historiques des Princes* in which he listed his sources. Henceforth, for esthetic reasons stories were set in a realistic and historical context.[2] The first widely diffused work of this genre in France was *La Princesse de Clèves* written by Mme de Lafayette and first published in 1678. It is she, then, who is generally credited as having initiated the *nouvelle historique*. But even during the Classical period the nouvelle incorporated many of the elements of the older unrealistic *romance*.

In some of these nouvelles, then, history plays a minor role for, quite often, it is totally eclipsed by the fiction. In *La Princess de Montpensier* (published in 1662), for example, the historical references are extremely vague and general and indeed some research is required if one wishes to be able to date the important moments of the story, as this would not be evident from a simple reading of the text.[3] In Mme de Lafayette's *La Comtesse de Tende* (first published in 1724 but presumably written around 1663) history or even historical chronology fulfills, for all practical purposes, no function whatsoever. One can, from a *romanesque* perspective, inquire then as to why Mme de Lafayette chooses historical characters. She explains this choice in the *avis au lecteur* in the initial publication of *La Princesse de Montpensier*:

Cette histoire n'a estée tirée d'aucun manuscrit. . .L'auteur ayant voulu, pour son divertissement, écrire des aventures inventées à plaisir a jugé plus à propos de prendre des noms connus dans nos histoires que de se servir de ceux que l'on trouve dans les romans, croiant bien que la réputation de Madame de Montpensier ne seroit pas blessée par un récit effectivement fabuleux.[4]

This author appears to be following the advice of Segrais who in his *Nouvelles Françoises ou Les Divertissemens de la Princesse Aurélie* (1656) suggests that writers should select as the starting point of their fictions the princes and knights of France. According to her own account, Mme de Lafayette selects a few names from "nos histories" in order to bestow a certain air of credibility to her narration. Hence, she does not hesitate to create other purely fictional characters while openly fictionalizing even the historical ones.

It is in this vein that Mme de Villedieu in 1669 explores the famous personages of sixteenth-century France to compose her *Journal Amoureux*. In this text also, history is pseudo-history as most of the characters are highly fictionalized. The author writes in the *avis au lecteur*: "Encore qu'il y a beaucoup de noms illustres dans cette histoire qui la font croire véritable, il ne faut pas toutefois la regarder de cette manière. . . l'on n'y a inseré des noms connus que pour flatter plus agréablement vôtre imagination."[5]

Her next prose work, *Les Annales Galantes* (1670), seems a more concerted effort to write a different kind of nouvelle. Mme de Villedieu affirms that this work contains "la vérité historique dont je marque la source dans la table que j'y ai inserée au commencement de ce premier tome . . .ce sont des traits fidelles de l'Histoire Generale" [sic]. She feels forced to reveal, nevertheless, that she has "added" several "ornaments" to the simplicity of history:

La majesté des matières historiques ne permet pas à l'historien judicieux de s'étendre sur les incidents purement galants; il ne les rapporte qu'en passant. J'ai dispensé nos annales de cette austerité. . .j'augmente donc à l'histoire quelques entrevues secretes, quelques discours amoureux.

But most significantly, the novelist adds further that "si ce ne sont ceux qu'ils ont prononcés, ce sont ceux qu'ils auroient dû prononcer. Je n'ai point de mémoires plus fidèles que mon jugement . . . ."6

Mme de Villedieu argues that even though historical changes may be impelled by passions, the official historian can only allude to them in passing. His historical account therefore may be augmented with dialogues, encounters, and other "ornaments" to enhance its simplicity. By relying on her judgment, experience and knowledge of human nature, the writer can invent amorous intrigues without exceeding the boundaries of the humanly or the historically "possible." In *Les Annales Galantes*, consequently, fidelity to a predetermined psychological "truth" of human nature takes precedence over the accurance of the historical data.

In 1671 Mme de Villedieu gave her public *Amours des Grands Hommes* which contains seven separate stories in which the "history" exploited is closer to that of the author's own day; it is therefore more specific and more localized than in the earlier *Annales Galantes*. One finds in the 1671 text, for example, the story of Bussi d'Amboise.7 The seventeenth-century reader was more or less well informed about the period of the religious wars from the *mémoires* and *histoires* that inundated the first half of the seventeenth century.8 In spite of this, in *Les Amours des Grands Hommes*, Mme de Villedieu is a genuine fictionist.

In *Les Désordres de l'Amour* there is a perceptible change. Here, as this study has indicated, the text is faithfully and at times almost painstakingly documented. The nouvelles will provide the domonstration or proof of an axiom which is enunciated or inscribed before each story. History now is to function as an example of a transcendental "Truth"; hence, the more the facts of history are respected, the more forceful and efficacious the demonstration--and of course the demonstration seems particularly forceful in the case of the Valois court, where the political disorders had been so long in being rectified that their consequences could still be felt in the middle of the seventeenth century.[9] In showing that passions ruined not only the personal lives of their victims but that they were equally the source of the troubles that beleaguered the entire nation, Mme de Villedieu accords her work a certain moral dimension and at the same time creates, or rather *re*-creates, through her representation, the political drama and the personal trauma of that period. In this text the rules of historical casuality are never seriously sacrificed and the nouvelles never enter the domain of the pure *romanesque*.

Mme de Villedieu composes her nouvelles, therefore, in a fundamentally different way than does the author of *La Princesse de Clèves*. The latter mentions a historical event usually to illuminate one of her (oftentimes) invented characters and quite frequently she deforms the historical incident or interprets it solely in light of the episodes that she has imagined.[10] Historical fact or truth does not necessarily determine the psychology or behavior of the protagonists; for, in the final analysis, Mme de Lafayette exploits history in somewhat of a true *romanesque* tradition. For Mme de Villedieu, by contrast, the *nouvelle historique* is indeed historical; and, in her hands, the genre appears to assume a more serious note. The utilization of official history obliges the author to respect the *vrai* and no longer merely the *vraisemblable*.

Also, at the time that Mme de Villedieu was composing her prose works, the abbé de Saint-Réal published *Dom Carlos*, believed to be the first work subtitled *nouvelle historique*. The preceding year he had circulated his *De l'Usage de l'Histoire* in which he attempted to articulate and specify the goal of the historian:

> Etudier l'Histoire, c'est étudier les
> motifs, les opinions, et les passions des
> hommes, pour en conaître tous les ressorts
> et les détours, enfin toutes les illusions
> qu'elles savent faire aux esprits, et les
> surprises qu'elles font au coeur.[11]

In this nouvelle, Saint-Réal *over*-documents his work. Historical references abound in the preface and are even included in the margins of the text. Yet, the abbé himself seems to use history as a starting point for fiction because the images that he gives of the tragic destinies of Dom Carlos and Queen Elizabeth conform very little to the facts as they can be reconstructed from his own sources.[12] In effect, Saint-Réal takes a romance-like plot and "fattens" it with a new political twist. After the publication of this nouvelle (1672) the genre appears to have been exceedinly popular; but it began to re-incorporate the *romanesque* elements from the *nouvelle galante*.[13] In *Les Désordres de l'Amour*, as this study has attempted to show, one is confronted with a coherent and a historically accurate portrait of its sixteenth-century characters.

In addition to this difference between a Villedieu and a Saint-Réal in the utilization of historical matter, there are also differences in the mode of representation. The role of the narrator for these two writers also differentiates their works. Whereas, as one must conclude from the second part of this study, the "scene" is very essential in *Les Désordres de l'Amour*, it is non-existent in *Dom Carlos*. All dialogue in Saint-Réal's work is transposed in the indirect style and there are but six responses in direct discourse. The abbé fails to dramatize his narrative; and this very kind of dramatization is one of Mme de Villedieu's strongest traits. His narrator, never personalized, is monotonously the objective historian detached at all times from the narrated event and the text. Saint-Réal's nouvelle constitutes a true *énoncé historique* for there is a minimum of direct discursive intervention. In Mme de Villedieu's text, the narrator, as moralist, possesses a distinct personality.

Significantly, it can be noted that *Dom Carlos* is writen entirely in the *passé simple* whereas in *Les Désordres de l'Amour*, the present and perfect tenses constantly and strategically interweave into the fabric of the aoristic narrative.

** ** **

The Metaphoricity of the Classical Nouvelle

The *nouvelle historique* for Mme de Villedieu functions then as a kind of discourse on history that fragments the linearity of the past. And in fragmenting the *récit historique*, the *discours* of *Les Désordres de l'Amour* assures its own non-linearity. In fact, for each fragment of *récit* corresponds a fragment of *discours*. The text in its totality is extremely metaphorical; and this metaphoricity manifests itself on two levels: within each individual nouvelle as well as within the text *in toto*. One can identify the nouvelles in Mme de Villedieu's work both collectively and separately with what Jakobson has formulated as one of two aspects in any sign system: selection and combination.[14] To each of these corresponds a rhetorical device: metaphor (selection), as the substitution of one signifier for another having the same meaning; and metonymy (combination), as the gliding from one sign to another. "Esthétiquement, le recours dominant au procédé métaphorique fonde tous les arts de la variation; le recours au procédé métonymique fonde tous ceux du récit.[15]

Each nouvelle in *Les Désordres de l'Amour* is indeed constructed as a series of semantic equations having the same signified. The first nouvelle, for example, is divided into three prose segments that can all be reduced (semantically) to the axiom with which the story begins: "Que l'amour est le ressort de toutes les autres passions de l'âme." This is to say that the three segments are all variations and elaborations of

134

this *sententia*. Moreover, as was indicated in the second part of this study, the relationship between the three maxims in verse and the prose of the nouvelle to which they correspond is equally a metaphorical one.[16]

The characters in the first nouvelle are themselves substitutive and interchangeable without altering the structure of the story. Monsieur, the King of Navarre, the duc de Guise, and to a certain extent even Henri III--ignoring for the moment their historical positions and functions--are superposable within the psychological analysis of the text as Mme de Sauve's *lover*. In the permutating equation *amant/amante*, the first term alone changes during the progression of the plot; Mme de Sauve remains constant. Love has an identical effect on all of the suitors, and caught in the rages of passion, they are indistinguishable. The same is true for Mlle de Châteauneuf, Mlle d'Elbeuf, and Mme de Sauve as mistresses of the king.

In the second and third stories, one confronts precisely the same schema: the Maréchal de Termes and the baron de Bellegarde are both husbands of Marguerite; Bellegarde and Givry are both suitors of the princesse de Guise, etc.; and here too each nouvelle is divided into semantically equivalent prose segments. In fact, all of the characters in *Les Désordres de l'Amour* are metaphors for passion; and that is why even though the images or portraits presented of them are historically accurate and even though they are individualized and recognizable as "personalities" and are distinguishable in their political or social functions, their psychological or psychic individuality is merely one of degrees. In the world created by Mme de Villedieu, passion is the essence of mankind; and, in the final analysis, it can only be declined or conjugated in a pure succession.

However, not only is each nouvelle divided into semantic equations, but, as suggested earlier, the relationship between the three nouvelles themselves is metaphorical. Just as the first story is the result of the concatenation of a series of three equations, so, too, is *Les*

135

Désordres de l'Amour a series of three larger
equations each displaying the same signified. The
three stories are superposable and interchangeable. Taken together, they constitute variations
on a broader theme: *the disorders of love*.
Although there are three separate stories told
(or rather re-told from Mézeray's first telling),
the text is not, strictly speaking, in the realm
of the *récit* (in Roland Barthes' sense);[17] it is
an extended metaphor. Mme de Villedieu offers the
vocabulary or "lexicon," so to speak, of passion
under the collective rubric of *désordres*. As
Barthes has shown is true for La Bruyère, the
novelist here chooses episodes and events (war,
peace, royal divorce, etc.) that have the same
signified (passion) and collects them in a con-
tinuous metaphor. In spite of the unique character of each of the three stories, they are
components of a paradigmatic framework that is
never lost from sight when each particular one is
considered. Indeed, one would expect this from a
text that undertakes the demystification of the
past and its characters. "Le moralisme, qui est,
par définition, substitution des ressorts aux
apparences et des mobiles aux vertus, opère
d'ordinaire comme un vertige. . ."[18]

Les *Désordres de l'Amour* "defines" and
"illustrates" and is consequently a fragmented
text. It is one that fluctuates between the definition and the illustration; it is the intermediary between, or rather the combination of, the
maxim--pure metaphor, since it defines--and anecdote, pure *récit*. The novelist proposes one definition of human nature and attempts several demon-
strations but aborts them before they become
genuine *récit* (anecdote). Significantly, prior to
the publication of *Les Désordres de l'Amour*, Mme
de Mme de Villedieu had exploited fully neither
the shorter form of the nouvelle nor that of the
intervening maxim. Once she found her formula,
however, she could only repeat it with slight
variations: $Nouvelle_1 = Nouvelle_2 = Nouvelle_3$,
etc.

One could conclude from this that several
basic assumptions underlie Mme de Villedieu's use
and manipulation of history. It would appear that
historical events, by their very nature, are never

unique; they repeat themselves. Or inversely, one might conclude that the future will always re-semble the past--or that which is repeated is historical for any constant repetition must possess a general signification:

> In history. . .there is an endless variety of instances which fall under roughly the same general description. . .part of the fascination of history lies in this spec-tacle of an innumerable variety of qualita-tively different actions and passions, exhibited by human beings down the ages, which are for all that still instances of the same general description, and are covered by the same general principles. . . which if enunciated, come in the end to be little more than truisms.[19]

1. Montaigne, *Essais*, II, 25; ed. M. Guillbaud, 1962, p. 139.

2. Many studies mark the growth of historical realism in the seventeenth-century novel:

> Dorothy Dallas, *Le Roman Français de 1660-1680* (Paris: Gamber, 1932).

> George May, *Le Dilemme du Roman* (New Haven: Yale University Press, 1963); and "L' Histoire a-t-elle engendré le Roman" in *Revue de l'Histoire Littéraire de la France*, LV (1955), 155-176.

> Moses Ratner, *Theory and Criticism of the Novel In France from Astrée to 1750* (New York: n.p., 1937).

> Marie-A. Raynal, *Le Talent Nouveau de Mme de Lafayette* (Paris: Picart, 1927).

Barbara Woshinsky, in her short study of *La Princesse de Clèves*, best recapitulates the findings of these works:

> . . .already before the classical period authors of romance made historical claims for their works. As early as 1661, La Calprenède dissociated himself from the *auteurs de romans*. Speaking of his earlier works, he claimed they were not romances but histories. . .Although his historical assertions are greatly exaggerated, a gradual 'historization' did indeed take place within the romance genre. While all 17th century romances were essentially non-realistic, certain gradations are apparent in their non-realism. A medieval chivalric romance

like *Amadis de Gaule.* . . .possessed the vaguest of geographical and temporal set- tings. *L'Astrée* (1607-1627), while its characters and events belong to the conven- tional fantasy-world of the pastoral, does take place at a definite time--between 450- 475 A.D.--and in a real setting, D'Urfé's own *pays du forez*. The next fictional generation, which includes Gomberville and Desmarets de St-Sorlin, weaved its romances around real figures taken from ancient history. Despite their flagrant trespasses against historical truth, these writers did situate their works at fairly precise moments in history. Moreover, they treated historical periods which came closer and closer to the present time.

During the 1660's while the Scudérys were still writing their historical *romans à clé* (*Clélie*, 1654-1660; *Almahide, 1660-1663*) . . .a new form, the nouvelle historique, began to gain favor. . . (pp. 54-55)

The 1660's also saw the republications of several sixteenth-century memoirs and historical texts which inspired several works of fiction dealing with the religious wars during the Valois rule: Mme de Lafayette's *Princesse de Montpensier* (1662), for example. It was, more precisely, the 1670's that saw the *nouvelle historique* flourish as a genre.

3. Thus, for example, in Mme de Lafayette's first nouvelle it is a fact that the princess' marriage took place in 1566 so one can date her meeting (in the novel) with the duc de Guise as 1569, etc.

4. Mme de Lafayette, *Romans et Nouvelles,* ed. E. Magne (Paris: Garnier, 1961), p. 3.

5. *Le Journal Amoureux*, Barbin, 1669, 6 vol.

6. Mme de Villedieu continues:

. . .quand on m'en fournira quelques [mémoires], où mes Heros parleront mieux que dans mes Annales, je consens à rapporter leurs paroles propres. Mais tant que les Historiens les rendront *muets*, je croiray pouvoir les faire parler à ma mode. Mais sans craindre de nous écarter davantage du droit chemin, nous pouvons toûjours mêler un peu d'amour aux incidens qui nous paroissent les plus éloignez de cette passion; car à prendre bien les choses, il n'y a guere d' avanture, quelque tragique qu'elle paroisse, dont les Annales Galantes ne peussent devenir la chronologie historique. (Avant-propos, *Annales Galantes* in *Oeuvres de Mme de Villedieu*, 1702, t. II) (emphasis added)

7. This is the same sixteenth-century Bussi that is a character in the second nouvelle of *Les Désordres de l'Amour*.

8. For a complete list of the works published, consult the bibliography of René Démoris, *Le Roman à la Première Personne* (Paris: Armand Colin, 1975).

9. Cuénin, introduction.

10. Francillon. See also article by Chamard and Rudler, "Les Sources Historiques de *La Princesse de Clèves*" in *Revue du Seizième Sicèle*, II (1914), 92-131; 289-291.

11. Saint-Réal, *De l'Usage de l'Histoire*, in *Oeuvres Complètes* (Paris: Nyon, 1745), VII, 314.

12. See Francillon's comments on Saint-Réal, "Mme de Lafayette et Saint-Réal," in *L'Oeuvre Romanesque de Mme de Lafayette*, pp. 276-277.

13. *Le Prince de Condé, nouvelle historique* by E. Boursault (1675), is an example of the mixing of these two different genres. In it the career of Condé (who under Francois II and Charles IX was head of the Protestant party) is seen only in light of his love adventures. See note 12 above.

14. Roman Jakobson, "Two Aspects of Language and Two Types of Aphasia," in Jakobsen and Halle, *Fundamentals of Language* (The Hague: Mouton,

1956), pp. 52-82.

15. Roland Barthes, *Essais Critiques* (Paris: Seuil, 1964), p. 233.

16. See above, Part II: ÉNONCIATION

17. I am taking "récit" here to mean narration of a "life" (from birth to death). Mme de Villedieu "isolates" certain moments of a life and ignores the rest. From the nouvelles one never knows, for example, *what happens* subsequently to Mme de Sauve, to the duc de Guise, or to Mme de Termes-Bellegarde, etc. Even Mme de Lafayette, through flashback and projection recounts the entire life of the princesse de Clèves.

18. Barthes, *Essais Critiques*, p. 231.

19. Arthur C. Danto, *Analytical Philosophy of History* (Cambridge: The University Press, 1965), p. 238.

CHAPTER FIVE

FROM *HISTOIRE* TO *NOUVELLE:*

THE "VERTICAL DEPTH" OF HISTORY

To raise the question of the *difference* between the representation of the series of events in the historical document and these same events in the nouvelles by Mme de Villedieu, as I have done in Chapters One and Two, is to raise ultimately the question of the production of the text. When Mme de Villedieu transforms the historical document into a nouvelle, not only in one particular instance has the center of gravity rotated from the king to his mistress (Nouvelle I), from politics to passion, as the power and influence of the crown succumb to those of love and jealousy, but the "status" of the narrated events or narration in relation to its recipient also changes.

Les Désordres de l'Amour is predicated upon the assumption that the reader is already familiar with the basic facts of history. An initial reading of the text confirms this; for if one is not, the nouvelles may appear at times rambling, confusing, or even incomplete and lacking in essential elements. For many of the events that require pages and pages of details and explanations in Mézeray, the nouvelle offers very little and sometimes no explanation at all.[1] For example, when the novelist writes of the "Catastrophe des Etats de Blois" (p. 120), she assumes that one is *au courant* and offers no further explanation. As a result, the cause and effect relationship of some political events appears to be absent in the nouvelle. But whereas in some of her other works (*Les Annales Galantes*, for example) Mme de Villedieu felt obliged to list her sources in order to justify their historicity, that is not the case in her 1675 text. History is now assumed to be common knowledge.

Les Désordres de l'Amour is much less a text about *what happened* than it is a text that attempts to postulate a "position" in relation to the past events; it is concerned less with the events of history than it is with itself as discourse. So the overriding question becomes no longer how to "represent" the events (referent: the sixteenth century) but how to choose and arrange the events of history so as to manifest or signify this position, this discourse (signified). The novelist is not content merely with exposing the facts of the past as perhaps would be the "historien judicieux"; she attempts to extract a transcendental Truth from this particular political truth. She puts history's characters and events on stage; they become examples. She shows and tells what happened (in the past); but in the process she shows and tells *what happens* (in the absolute). By directing her text less towards a slow unveiling of the past and more towards an immediate revelation and demystification of human nature in general (present as well as past), she has thereby shifted its balance away from the narrated event to the *one who narrates* and the *act of narrating*. The desire to demystify the present by means of historical examples has changed the angle and optic with which the past is contemplated. As a result, there are traces in the text of this shift in orientation that tend to overshadow the *chose racontée* itself.

Thus another way to speak of the movement from historical document to nouvelle in Mme de Villedieu's particular case is in terms of this displacement of emphasis from the *time* of the event to the *time* of its evocation and reception-- from the subject of the *énoncé*, the participants in the narrated event, to the subject and process of *énonciation*, the participants in the linguistic (or literary) event. In Benveniste's terminology one could perhaps formulate it as the movement where a *récit historique*--a text where there is a representation of the events with a minimum of intervention by the speaker or where his entire project is characterized by his attempt to erase the traces of his presence--modulates into a *discours*--a narrative where the speaker's presence is not only explicitly in evidence but where it is also the pivotal force of the text as he now attempts to persuade or influence his listener and not merely to "re-present." It is for this reason that one has been able to isolate so easily in *Les*

144

Désordres de l'Amour traces of the narrator's presence: i.e., the present tense and meta-narrative signs where he refers to himself and to his discourse to indicate its internal organization.

The nouvelle has a precise purpose: to uncover the hidden passions that form the basis for the important political facts and to extrapolate from this universal maxims on human behavior. Therefore, if the details as written in the documents are not ideal they must be re-read or *rearranged* in a different perspective by changing their relative emphasis so that what is parenthetical in the official document becomes principal in the nouvelle and vice versa. Therein, the nouvelle offers a new interpretation of the past; and this new interpretation is, in the final analysis, the result of a double activity, selection *and* combination.

In fact, all of the changes, extensions, or "speculations" found in the nouvelles can be reduced to these two operations. By adjusting or superimposing the nouvelles with the document that served as their principal inspiration, one is able to ascertain that Mme de Villedieu has effectuated a veritable *découpage* of the source. She isolates certain elements--people and events--and then *orders* them according to her own organizing principles, principles that assume a poetic representation within the text. It should be evident from the discussions above that human passion is the key to the combination with which these selected elements are transformed, substituted, and combined in the text. With this mechanism of organization, the novelist adds a force, an energy, thus a *signification* to history. Her text, in its totality, is to the events of the past what the *verb* is to the sentence. In a different perspective, one might say that she proposes a *grammar* for the events of history with which they *flow* and *mean*. Yet, much like a sentence itself, Mme de Villedieu's nouvelles are personal and creative; for indeed it is only after re-reading, or in this case a re-writing of history, that its meaning emerges.

145

** ** **

History and Literature:

Open-Ended and Closed Texts

The very fact that the *nouvelle historique* would undertake a restructuring of the past suggests that there is something missing in the historical document or that history by its very nature must necessarily be an incomplete, *porous* narrative. And if one uses *Histoire de France* and *Les Désordres de l'Amour* as typical examples of these genres, it would appear that history and the nouvelle were moving almost imperceptibly in opposite directions. This movement reflects perhaps a distinction that was made, at least implicitly, between two kinds of "historical" writings: on the one hand, history as an annal of the past (in the original meaning of "annal": a pure chronological order devoid of interpretive value); and, on the other hand, history as an elaboration of the past.[2] Such a distinction is, when magnified, that between history as a scientific exercise (the gathering of facts) and history as an artistic or literary enterprise (the interpretation of these facts for their emotional and intellectual value).[3] And in this perspective, it is interesting to note again the general orientation of Mézeray's *Histoire de France*. From a highly personal and somewhat dramatic narrative in the first volume (1643) which is slighly attenuated in the second (1646), this seventeenth-century historian in his last volume (1651) de-dramatizes and de-personalizes his work to a great extent. His *Histoire* finally and symptomatically evolves into his *Abrégé Chronologique ou extrait de l'Histoire de France*--a movement towards a pure chronology.[4]

Yet, already in the third volume of the *Histoire de France*, there is a perceptible suppression of the first person pronouns *je* and *nous*. Also conspicuously absent is the use of dialogue in the direct style; furthermore, general maxims or observations on human behavior are indeed a

146

rara avis. And the third volume of Mézeray's *Histoire*, again symbolically, is the only one that displays for each paragraph of the text marginal notations that *date* the succession of the events year by year. These notations were added after the completion of the text and the historian draws his reader's attention to these veritable *chronograms*:

> L'Auteur avoit creu avoir de grandes raisons de ne point marquer ainsi les années dans ses deux premiers volumes, mais tout consideré, il a trouvé qu'il y en avoit encore de plus grandes de le faire. (III, 1)

One could venture to affirm that this final and explicitly chronogrammatic volume, from which Mme de Mme de Villedieu acquires the bulk of her materials, is not designed to assign categorically a meaning to the past; nor perhaps is it designed to discourse in general terms on human behavior to the same extent as were perhaps the previous two. Yet the narrative does this more or less because its structure permits a certain latitude or freedom within which the reader can "circulate" and formulate his own conclusions. The text has the appearances of being somewhat open-ended.

Les Désordres de l'Amour, on the contrary, by filling in the "meaning" of history is a closed text. The reader does not and can not feel that he has independently defined or discovered the general axioms in question: the "lesson" here is not dissolved or diluted into the total representation; it is presented instead in its concentrated and unadulterated form. From her earlier "historical" works to *Les Désordres de l'Amour*, Mme de Villedieu proceeds in the opposite direction from a Mézeray and toward a more personalization and dramatization of her narratives. Not only is the "Truth" categorically stated by the mediating voice, it is held under a magnifying lens.

** ** **

Histoire and *Nouvelle*: from a Classical
Perspective

In the Classical perspective then, if
history (as chronicle) is an attempt to signify
the continuity of the past, the *nouvelle histori-*
que, somewhat antagonistically, effectuates, symbolically at least, its discontinuity. Both novelist and historian would treat ultimately the
relationship of private life to public function;
but whereas the themes and methods of the latter
would be concerned basically with the problem of
the *flow* of past occurrences--namely, how to indicate the historical progression from event "A" to
event "B"--those of the former would concern themselves principally with the demystification of
past occurrences--i.e., how to account for event
"A".

Again, in this Classical perspective, the
"causes" of past events for the historian would be
revealed through a slow process of *accretion*; for
the novelist they would reveal themselves through
violent, dramatic, and immediate *revelations*. The
past in the historical document thus would be
given a shape designed ultimately to show time;
its form would be that of developing thought.[5] As
Mézeray himself proclaims, "sa beauté consiste
[rait] plus en la matière qu'en la forme, et. . .
tous les sujets y étant illustrez et révelez, on y
considere[rait] plustôt le génie de ceux qui
agissent, que de celui qui représente les actions"
(*Histoire*, III, *Epitre dédicatoire*).

The historian's product, as it would follow
above all else a chronological structure, would
result in the treatment of the individual and his
society and institutions that would remain static
and fixed in the past. Consequently, some of the
events in his work may appear isolated, connected
only by the chronology since the historian would
try to order all those events that occurred within
a particular time span and within a precise geographical entity, even though otherwise these

events may be quite dissimilar or even unrelated.[6] Thus the historical narrative as a whole might appear non-dramatic or perhaps even anti-dramatic. Here, where the establishment of "Truth" is not so much the effect of an arrangement as it is a representation of the facts in their natural synchrony, the narrative voice should be limited and tempered (rare use of the first person and the present tense) as the sole commentator on history is the chronology itself.[7] Furthermore, there would abound in the historical record (as indeed one does find in Mézeray) page after page of details specifying military tactics and maneuvers, the provisions of treaties, etc., and although the historian may suggest that private motives rather than public interest compose the forces behind the events, he could never analyze these forces. Thus, his narrative would lack vitality. The historical events are to be enunciated in the "modalities" of the king ('le roi vit que. . .," "le roi pensa que. . .," "le roi dit que. . .," etc.); they are to be written principally in a political perspective and are to receive a documentary order, a temporal continuity.

The writer of "literature," on the other hand, would treat the problems of the individual and his society as they transcend historical time. These problems would no longer be static and isolated but would be dynamic and would entertain a rapport with the present. Consequently, the technical concerns about the narrative progression would become complicated with those geared towards the articulation of the discursive stance. The tendency here then would indeed be directly opposed to that of the historian whose efforts should be designed to minimize the esthetic devices that could possibly impede the representation of the occurrence. On the contrary, the narrative voice will now manipulate and control, sometimes surreptitiously, the selection and arrangement of the devices to represent the event. The nouvelle, at the outset, therefore, will postulate an interplay between the narrator and the narrated. The impartial narrator in history is replaced by a partisan one who functions to formulate a political norm and a moral code. The emphasis shifts away from chronology to themes and away from pure representation to *interpretation* in order to include the past in a present perspective and in a total vision. Thus the nouvelle will hinge upon a relationship between the text and its recipient as well as between the text and its initiator.

Again, in this Classical perspective, if the historian is to accord history a form, the novelist invests it with an *elaboration*; and if the past for the first is pre-eminently knowledge, for the second it is example. Hence, the nouvelle would constitute the place where the *passé simple* of fact could be supplemented with the present of commentary. Thus, Mme de Villedieu, as novelist, appears to be working from the premise that the past, as an enormous mass of sometimes unrelated parts, possesses no intrinsic coherence, no inherent signification. Therefore, a coherence or *order* must be extracted from, or more precisely, embedded into it. The function of the nouvelle would consist in providing a coherence for the past; for, as a text, it would coordinate what would have otherwise remained the confusion of historical data. It acts thereby as a "corrective" for this confusion, transforming it into "categories of comprehension." This ordering of the past would result from a process of generalization that the nouvelle effectuates and whereby the text displays all of the examples of the past. It would be these generalizations derived from history that would constitute a kind of grammar of human experience and activity.[8] Moreover, one could conclude from *Les Désordres de l'Amour* that the novelist assumes that the past is in no way unique since the moral principles that explicate it remain unchanged for all times and places. The nouvelle provides a guide not only for perceiving and comprehending the past, it also constitutes a guide for the present.

If the historian is to reveal the temporal continuity of past events, the novelist is to provide history with a different kind of continuity-- one that is atemporal as it is bound to no particular time. In Mme de Villedieu's case, the disorders of the sixteenth century are no longer exposed simply in terms of political causes but are reduced further to the irrational and sometimes unconscious sentimental causes. The pragmatism of the political is supplanted by the rage and

150

fanaticism of the passional.

In the *nouvelle historique*, insofar as Mme de Villedieu undertook to write it, the process of signification is an attempt to formulate and articulate a meaning for history. The writer sees herself perhaps not so much as collecting facts as selecting *signifiers* (for passion). She then arranges these signifiers of historical disorders so as to produce a definitive signification: i.e., all political activity finds its basis in human passion and in love in particular. Her text, by virtue of its very structure, is to propose an ideological elaboration of the past.

Objective history (impossible though it may be, but which would approach its closest realization in a pure chronology) to the Classical thinker might resemble somewhat a sign reduced to two terms: the signifier and the referent. (Again, I use "sign" here not in its strictly Saussurean sense but in its larger metaphorical sense: history as a sign; fiction as a sign with a referent, a signifier [words, phrases, the text *grosso modo*], and a signified [e. g. meaning]). To be objective, the signified has to remain precisely unformulated and hidden in a sense behind the referent. This fusion of the referent and the signified constitutes what has been called "*l'effet du réel*": namely, the elimination of the signified out of objective narration by allowing the "real" and its expression to come into direct contact.[9]

The *nouvelle historique*, again as it finds its Classical articulation in *Les Désordres de l'Amour*, was to be viewed, as the analysis in the preceding chapters demonstrates, as the formulation of this implied signified (the codification of this "*effet du réel*") and was to be valued over official history. It includes precisely what the "historien judicieux" (as writes Mme de Villedieu) must ignore or must allude to only in passing. It is in this way that the nouvelle adds a vertical depth or paradigmatic elaboration of history. It constitutes a sign exhibiting three terms: signifier, referent, and signified. The *nouvelle historique* was to be valued equally over pure fiction, in this Classical perspective, because the facts and characters in the nouvelle enjoy *more* than just a linguistic existence (as a term of discourse). This second existence is rather the faithful "copy" or mimesis of the real so that the lessons presented here have an impressive and powerful impact.[10]

Yet, for the modern reader, the difference that Mme de Villedieu perceived between the historical narrative and her own project (a difference reflected by the distance between "mere" history and an elaboration of history) is more apparent than real. Seventeenth-century history, even if it were only a pure chronology, contains, as specified above, a signified. Mézeray's text has a "meaning"; and although it is not always rendered as unmistakingly explicit as it appears in Mme de Villedieu's narrative, this meaning is nonetheless unequivocal and sometimes unabated. His *Histoire de France* quite obviously was composed to serve as an example. One might best characterize the relationship between Classical history and the *nouvelle historique*, or more correctly between *Histoire de France* and *Les Désordres de l'Amour*, in terms of what has been formulated elsewhere as two theories in a kind of philosophy of history.[11] The substantive philosophy of history attempts to discover either a *descriptive* or an *explanatory* theory to account for the past. Mézeray's text, as a descriptive theory, seeks to reveal a particular pattern or cycle in the historical events. There exists perhaps an implicit claim here that subsequent events will probably constitute a repetition of the cycle. *Les Désordres de l'Amour* attempts to supersede this descriptive theory by accounting for it in causal terms. It is descriptive because, like the historical narrative, it too specifies a pattern, i.e., it is inalterably the actions of great men and women that propel the historical events; it is explanatory inasmuch as the nouvelle seeks to identify the causation (passions) behind the pattern. Here, there is the explicit claim that future events can only repeat or complete the cycle. Furthermore, one is to assume that the pattern would cease if ever the causative forces should become inoperative; the nouvelle, however, does not suggest that this will ever be the case as it would require a kind of utopia where men could control their passions instead of being controlled by them.

The nouvelle, as opposed to history, is, in this respect, concerned not only with the past but with the entire future as well. In the historical narrative, a particular event has a meaning *vis à vis* the larger temporal structure of which it is a component; in the nouvelle the events and the past in general are assigned a meaning in a non-historical context. The essence of the past, in other words, depends upon an atemporal reality. Mme de Villedieu took such care to write an "accurate" account because, like the historian, she wanted the final product to be useful; but she wanted it to be serviceable in a different way. Whereas *Histoire de France* seems to be aimed foremost at anyone interested in learning what happened in the past, *Les Désordres de l'Amour* is functional in a non-historical way in that Mme de Villedieu's purpose for writing a historical account in the first place is basically non-historical. The nouvelles are a guide for all times; they surpass a mere relation of what transpired. By availing herself of three very forceful examples, the novelist can explain, from these instances of disorders, all disorders--past, present, and future. It is for these reasons that the novelist has suggested, as this study has indicated, that human motivations are everywhere and always the same. It is equally for these reasons that her conclusions are meant to be independent of time and that the reader is to see himself mirrored in the text.[12]

** ** **

Both history and the *nouvelle historique* exploit the example (I am referring here, of course, to the *exemplum* as a literary device); in the first case, "history" is written and (it is supposed) ultimately constitutes an example; whereas in the second, the example is written to consti-

tute or include "history."[13] In the first
instance, the pragmatic significance or moral
principle of the narrative is the conclusion that
the reader forms; in the second, it is the opening
phrase of the text itself.

Apropos of the three specific histories in
question, in history as example, the events are
enunciated according to their syntagmatic connection; in the example as history, in their paradigmatic relation. The difference has been formulated elsewhere as one between the narrative and
the systematic disposition of texts.[14] In the
movement from history to nouvelle, the narrative
scheme (which in history is *developed* in syntagmatic form) is *reduced* in the nouvelle to paradigmatic categories. This is what I mean when I
contend that chronology is subordinated to a thematic organization.

If the anecdote (fable *and* historical example in the Aristotelian sense) is the minimal
narrative form that is derived from minimal systematic forms (the moral principle, the *sententia*)
then the *nouvelle historique*, as somewhat of a
boundary between systematic texts and narrative
texts, should be, as indeed *Les Désordres de
l'Amour* is, a combination of the maxim and the
anecdote. It is where the smallest systematic
unit enters into a precise relationship with the
smallest narrative unit. This present study has
attempted, furthermore, to explore how a systematic form or a moral axiom is expanded to produce a
narrative text--an expansion, in my estimation,
that fails to become fully actualized. The relation between the maxim and the prose in Mme de
Villedieu's nouvelles is not unique but attests
rather to what would be found to some extent in
the constitution of any story that forms part of a
moral system: "Toute histoire est caracterisée
par un déséquilibre spécifique dans l'expansion
narrative qui provient lui-même de la connexion
pragmatique. . .dont relève l'histoire."[15]

Thus, in the final analysis, the nouvelle is
both an expansion and a reduction: expansion in
relation to the maxim upon which it is founded;
reduction in relation to the history (or
histories) with which the maxim is particular-

ized.[16] It is precisely because "history" in the *nouvelle historique* is composed explicitly and deliberately from a moral perspective that it appears detached from the historical continuum and that it contains its meaning in itself. It is the exemplary genre *par excellence*.[17]

In history as example, the moral principle of the historian which (necessarily) determines and organizes the narrative, is purported to be absent; in the example as history it is omnipresent. Thus, in the *nouvelle historique*, the example itself is problematic in the sense that the nouvelle problematizes, as one can determine from the second part of this study, the relationship between the prose and the moral verse. From the first to the last poetic axiom, one remarks a "distancing" in the degree of correspondence between the principle and its expansion.

The nouvelles are oriented in such a way that it is the intervention of the narrator-historian at different textual levels that constitutes and reveals the essence of the past, of history itself. The majesty of the example emanates less from the historical events than from the historian's ability to (re)organize and (re) evaluate the events. Simply stated, the process by which Mme de Villedieu progresses from history as example to example as history, that is to say, from historical document to nouvelle, is by means of the problematic example where by the moral implications of the document are developed and explicated in the narrative scheme itself.

During the course of this study, I have metaphorically characterized *Les Désordres de l'Amour*--this fragmented mixture of prose and poetry, of maxim and anecdote--as a text where the *récit historique* is punctuated with *discours*; as one where history is fragmented to permit the crystallization of its signification; as one where *Histoire* modulates into *nouvelle historique*. And finally, in this optic Mme de Villedieu's perceptive estimation of the direction and the essence of her own project assumes its full significance with perhaps a particular nuance for the modern reader:

> *J'augment* donc à l'histoire quelques *entre-*
> *vues* secretes, quelques *discours* amoureux.
> (emphasis added)

> (*Les Annales Galantes*, 1670)

It is as if

> "*L'art seul et non la science peut finale-*
> *ment nous donner des images d'ensemble.*"

> (H. Hoffding, *La Pensée Humaine*, 1911)

NOTES

CHAPTER FIVE

1. Mézeray's explanation of Monsieur's escape, for example, vol. III, pp. 1-32.

2. Danto, *Analytical Philosophy of History*.

3. This distinction between history and chronicle (or *mere* chronicle and history), as Danto in his *Analytical Philosophy of History* has convincingly argued, is perhaps one that in some respects can not be easily maintained. First of all, it is a distinction predicated upon the existence of an "ideal imitation" or a perfect account of the past from which the historian is to subsequently devise an interpretation. In the sense that a pure description of the past devoid of and independent from any interpretative value is impossible, history or the work of the historian can not be so divided. Even a representation of the past that has been reduced to a pure chronology employs an "over-arching connection" (p. 238).

Yet this distinction between mere chronicle and "true" history is sometimes found in some of the philosophical writings on history (e.g., Benedetto Croce, *History--Its Theory and Practice*). Here, chronicle is defined as an account of what happened and nothing more and history as the ascription of meaning to the reported facts. Danto maintains that a historical narrative can only tell precisely "what happened"; and to the extent that it does something else, it becomes more than historical. The historical account could be given an explicit pragmatic significance, for example. It is perhaps in this vein that one is to understand the distinction that would prompt a seventeenth-century novelist to undertake a rewriting of history.

4. It is obvious that Mézeray was dissatisfied with what he considered the faults of his *Histoire de France*. "Il se proposa une réédition où il pourrait se servir des connaissances qu'il avait acquises sur la méthode historique" (Evans,

Mezéray l'Historien, p. 69). His ideas on what a history should be are formulated more or less in the manuscript "Dessein d'une Parfaite Histoire de France" (for which the date of composition is unknown but which quite obviously post-dates his *Histoire*). It was to be "une Histoire des François non pas de la France ny des Rois de France, ny de la monarchie françoise pource que je donnerois toutes les gestes François aussi bien dedans que dehors la France. . ." (quoted by Evans, p. 71).

This project, however, was never realized; instead the historian worked for several years and published in 1668 his *Abrégé* (which Evans considers to be more a general history of Europe or perhaps even a universal history). After the *Abrégé* and his subsequent censure by Colbert, Mézeray published only one additional work, *l'Origine des François ou l'Histoire de France avant Clovis*. In this instance, he chose a subject so removed in time so as to offend no one. Moreover, he attempted merely to present the facts and to leave the task of drawing conclusions to the reader himself. In the *avertissement* he writes:

> Les lecteurs pourront remarquer dans ce Volume, comme dans les autres, le même air de sincerité et de désintéressement qui a rendu leur auteur célèbre. . .il juge des histories. . .comme en ont jugé les personnes les plus désintéressées. (Cited by Evans, p. 78)

5. Braudy, *Narrative Form in History and Fiction*.

6. This is what Braudy declares to be the case for the historian Hume, for example. And Mézeray writes in the preface to his *Histoire*:

> La distribution de mon ouvrage n'est point par Sections, ni par Chapitres: j'ay creu que toutes ces découpures gâtoient l'étoffe . . .La Chronologie y est bien marquée pour les principales actions; Et pour les autres, je les ay rangées avec une telle suite,

qu' encore qu'on ne lise pas les années en marge, on peut néanmoins *nécessairement* inférer de ma narration.

7. Roland Barthes, "Le Discours de l'Histoire," in *Social Science Information*, VI-2/3 (April-June 1967).

8. Braudy, *Narrative Form in History and Fiction*, p. 27.

9. Barthes, "Le Discours de l'Histoire"

10. Thus pure fiction, like objective history, might appear to be a sign reduced to two terms: signifier and signified. There is no referent in the sense that it is imaginary or "phantom."

Aristotle in the *Rhetoric* formulates precisely the same distinction between fiction (fable) and the historical example in any discourse that attempts to persuade:

> Les fables conviennent à la harangue et elles ont cet avantage que s'il est difficile de trouver des faits réellement arrivés qui soient tous pareils, il est plus facile d'imaginer des fables. . .Les arguments par les fables sont plus faciles à se procurer; mais les arguments par les faits historiques sont plus utiles pour la déliberation; car le plus souvent l'avenir ressemble au passé.
>
> (1393a, trans. by M. Dufour, Paris, 1973, and cited by K. Stierle (see above p. 46, note 34), p. 187.

11. Danto, *Analytical Philosophy of History*.

12. This is what Danto terms the "prophecy" of substantive philosophies of history which is "not merely a statement about the future (as too is a prediction); it is a *historical* statement about the future" (p. 14). Furthermore, he maintains that a substantive philosophy of history is a mis-

159

conceived activity that rests upon a basic error: "it is a mistake. . .to suppose that we can write the history of events before the events themselves have happened" (p. 14).

13. This opposition, history as example and example as history, I borrow from K. Stierle, "L'Histoire comme Exemple, Exemple comme Histoire."

14. This distinction between narrative and systematic texts reflects an inherent duplicity of language itself which is both a "system" and a "process." Language as system is determined by the correlation of "or. . .or"; and as process, by "and. . .and."

La différence fondamentale qui sépare la langue comme procès et la langue comme système, la dimension syntagmatique et la dimension paradigmatique, cette différence se manifeste une seconde fois sur le plan des textes, dans la dimension de la langue comme procès, sous forme de différence entre textes systématiques et textes narratifs." (Stierle, p. 179)

15. Ibid., p. 184.

16. In a different context, this is how Stierle defines the historical example.

17. Stierle writes:

C'est seulement dans la mesure où les histoires prennent place dans [un] système moral et représentent l'un de ses éléments qu'elle peuvent acquérir une signification exemplaire, et c'est à cette seule condition qu'elles peuvent prétendre être soustraites au continuum du simple déroulement historique. . .et s'intégrer à un context nouveau, celui de la convergence paradigmatique d'histoires relativement à leur place à l'intérieur du système moral." (Ibid., p. 184)

APPENDIX

APPENDIX A

NOUVELLE I

Henri III's love for the princesse de Condé is regarded unfavorably by his mother who considers the princess too "experienced" for the young king. She endeavors, therefore, to use all of the beautiful ladies of the court to divert the monarch from this passion. She employs principally the services of three such "belles": Mlle de Châteauneuf, who previously had enjoyed the "favor" of the king; the princess d'Elbeuf; and the widow, Mme de Sauve, who was called, and justly so, the "most charming lady in all of France."

When the princesse de Condé expires unexpectedly, Henri is extremely distraught; there is even fear for his life as such is the extent of his depression. The three aforementioned ladies double their efforts to comfort the king; but only Mme de Sauve succeeds in winning him over. In fact, she eventually possesses such a "power" over the young king that the queen mother uses this influence to persuade Henri to marry the princesse de Vaudemont.

Mme de Sauve is such a beautiful creature ("elle surpassait en magnificence les personnes de la plus haute qualité") that every gentleman at court feels compelled to make known to her that he is somewhat affected by this beauty. One of her first admirers and lovers is the duc de Guise. Realizing that his mistress is constantly entertaining other admirers, however, the duke becomes so violently disappointed and jealous that he is driven to tactics of vengeance resembling those of warfare.

At about the same time, Mlle d'Elbeuf, who resents Mme de Sauve for having usurped the king's heart, allies herself with Mlle de Châteauneuf (who had the same complaint) in order to discredit Mme de Sauve. They engage the Queen of Navarre in their plans; and it is into this league of women that the duc de Guise enters to avenge the blows to his ego. This group succeeds in exciting a "storm" against Mme de Sauve.

The king of Navarre, in the meantime, falls in love with Mlle de Châteauneuf; and it is Guise who suggests that the "league" exploit this to its advantage. Mlle de Châteauneuf consents to feign interest in Navarre (in order to advance their cabal against Mme de Sauve) promising the king that there is nothing she would not accord him if he joined their conspiracy. She, of course, has no intentions of keeping her word.

Initially, Navarre, who is a naturally honest man, cannot resolve himself to do a disservice to a woman who has done him no harm. But he is in love and the pronouncements of Mlle de Châteauneuf constitute divine law; so he is persuaded to pretend to be in love with Mme de Sauve and agrees to insult her publicly once he has obtained her "favors."

Unfortunately for the conspirators, the King of Navarre does not capture the eye of Mme de Sauve. Unaware of this plot, the queen mother, who wishes to pacify Navarre for political reasons, orders Mme de Sauve to treat him more favorably. And thus it is that the most charming woman in all of France begins to fall into the trap set for her.

In the process, however, Navarre actually does fall in love with Mme de Sauve (such is her power) but decides to keep this a secret from all except the new object of his desire. His true feelings are finally discovered by the conspirators.

As Mme de Sauve is so beautiful, she attracts as well the attention of the King's (Henri's) brother, Monsieur. Cognizant of this passion, the duc de Guise resolves to create such a violent jealousy between Monsieur and the King of Navarre that Henri III will find it necessary to banish the cause of this conflict.

Realizing the precariousness of the position in which she finds herself and realizing that the duc de Guise is responsible, Mme de Sauve decides to wage her own "war" against him. To do this, she attempts to reconcile and re-kindle the affair with her former lover. She begins, with a totally affected attitude of conciliation, to flirt openly with and to flatter the duke. Guise is all too aware, however, of her dissimulations--boasting even to Mme de Sauve's enemies that he would resist even a sincere return of her affections just as now he is resisting this false one.

But when she finally succeeds in obtaining a private interview with the duke, Mme de Sauve pleads her case so effectively (complete with simulated tears) that he forgets all of his stern resolutions. Indeed, he leaves this interview so convinced of her "love" that he would have thought it criminal to believe otherwise.

For political reasons (to remain in the good graces of Monsieur), Guise proposes that he and his mistress hide their reconciliation and con-tinue to feign discord before the court members. Consequently, he publicly continues his asso-ciation with Mme de Sauve's enemies--using his knowledge to sabotage their plots--while privately he enjoys all of the privileges of her company. So it is that the duc de Guise considers himself to be leading the sweetest and most convenient life that a lover could possibly desire.

The truth of this reconciliation between the lovers is inadvertently discovered (by a certain M. Dugua who is Guise's rival for the king's con-sideration). Of all of Mme de Sauve's enemies, the Queen of Navarre appears most offended by Guise's betrayal and vows to seek revenge. She accidentally intercepts a letter written by the duke to Mme de Sauve in which she (the Queen of Navarre) and Monsieur are implicated. She deli-vers this letter to Monsieur which angers him so much that his former and dormant dislike for the Guises is re-activated. This prompts him to leave the court in order to equip himself with an army powerful enough to overwhelm the Guises.

For some time now, the prince de Condé and other Protestant leaders had been urging Monsieur to avenge the Saint Bartholomew Massacre; but, as he was a pacifist, he had always refused. Mme de

Sauve's letter, however, furnishes legitimate and sufficient reasons for revenge. His subsequent escape from court causes much confusion.

The queen mother, again politically motivated and again with the assistance of Mme de Sauve, embarks upon a journey to bring about Monsieur's return. Monsieur, recognizing Mme de Sauve to be the flirt that she is ("une coquette qui menageoit cinq ou six intrigues à la fois") has a genuine resentment against her. Moreover, having uncovered her previous pretenses, he would surely never trust her again. But the beautiful Mme de Sauve has such a "power" over the hearts and minds of her lovers that the mere sight of her easily changes any resolutions against her.

Therefore, with the greatest of facility, she persuades Monsieur that the letter in question is a ploy on the part of Guise to create trouble between them. Monsieur is totally convinced; and he is so pleased that he agrees to a six-month truce.

The King of Navarre had already been informed by his wife, the queen, of the reconciliation between the duc de Guise and his mistress; and fearing more betrayals, he also leaves the court.

The queen mother now employs Mme de Sauve to convince Navarre that her new affair with Guise is merely a political ploy to arrest the plots against her. Mme de Sauve attempts to do this by means of a letter; Navarre, however, proves more difficult to persuade than Monsieur as he remains "absent" from Mme de Sauve and does not have to contend with her physical "presence."

This letter to Navarre falls into Guise's possession; and upon discovering the treason and dissimulations of Mme de Sauve, he is overtaken with jealousy. He curses himself for being blind for so long; and resolving to punish the "coquette" for her perfidies, he sends to the King of Navarre copies of other letters written to him (Guise) by Mme de Sauve so that the king might see how this flirt has manipulated the two of them. And finally, Guise, as if he were engaged in a veritably declared war against his former mistress, sends to her a threatening letter exposing his vengeful intentions.

When Monsieur is finally made aware of Mme de Sauve's ultimate "crimes," he goes back on his promise for a cease-fire so that the civil war becomes more escalated and more partisan than ever before.

NOUVELLE II

The Marquis de Termes, son of the Maréchal de Termes, marries a young woman from Guyenne whom he learns to love only after their wedding, as he had never before seen her. The marquise responds honestly to all the efforts of tenderness on the part of her husband; and he has no reason to complain about her. But as he loves her with an *ardeur extrême*, he can be satisfied only with an equal and reciprocal passion. The more he tries to "inflame her heart," however, the more indifferent she seems.

Mme de Termes falls dangerously ill and although M. de Termes assembles the best known medical experts to attend his wife, they can diagnose but a "secret sadness" in her soul--a sadness of which the marquis is already aware but whose cause he has been unable to *penetrate*. He beseeches her to have confidence in him by revealing the cause of her ill-being, promising that he would do all within his power to remove the source of her tears. Mme de Termes can respond only with a *faux discours*; and her refusal to reveal the cause of her torment augments her husband's curiosity to such an extent that he is willing to resort to any means to penetrate the affair: he prays, he promises; he uses his authority as an officer and as her husband. Moreover, the more he attempts to moderate his curiosity the more intense it becomes.

Ultimately conceding to the wishes of her husband, Mme de Termes tells him what he wishes so to know. She confesses how since her childhood she has had a violent passion for his nephew, the baron de Bellegarde, who is equally in love with her. She further explains that although it is impossible for her to love anyone else, she would rather die than do anything unworthy of her husband's esteem. Consequently, she has forbidden the young Bellegarde from conversing with her directly ("une conversation particulière") or through letters.

The marquis is so surprised and so touched by this *discours* that he is incapable of interrupting it; and when he can no longer withstand this confession, he flees to his chambers. But M. de Termes is determined not to succumb to a state of depression. He loves his wife dearly; and after her, he loves his nephew more than anything else. Although he has just cause to be jealous and vengeful, he remains an honest and reasonable man in spite of the intensity of his passion. He considers the stars alone to be responsible for his misfortune.

Consequently, M. de Termes promises his wife that he will use all of his influence to dissolve their marriage. If successful, he promises, moreover, to arrange even her second marriage to his nephew; if he should be unable to dissolve their union, he will still renounce all of his rights as her husband as he will never again appear before her.

Determined to see his wife happy, the marquis seeks an audience with the king and would have in good faith kept his word; but fate does not accord him the opportunity. He is killed in the Battle of Jarnac.

In his will, the marquis declares that Mme de Termes (because of a default in consent) is not legally his spouse; and in order to compensate for this without denying his nephew's rights as heir, he decrees Bellegarde to be his sole heir with the stipulation, however, that the baron marry his widow.

This unusual will is published to the astonishment and the conclamation of the entire community (Guyenne). It is believed by some to be a forgery--with overtones of murder; others claim that it was not in the power of the deceased to make it. Still others, potential heirs themselves to the marquis' estate, conspire to prevent this marriage: they attempt to intercept the ecclesiastical dispensation authorizing the second marriage. Even Mme de Termes' father forbids his daughter to conclude this union and arranges so that the ceremony can not be performed in Guyenne.

Although she is initially concerned with her reputation and *gloire*, Mme de Termes slowly concedes to the wishes of her lover and consents in essence to her own kidnapping when it becomes clear that their marriage will never be sanctioned in Guyenne. They flee to another territory (Piedmont) where the first days of this union find the couple drunk with ecstasy. Bellegarde, renouncing his ambitions, opts to please his new bride to the detriment of his own *gloire*.

Although the marquise is undeniably the most beautiful woman of her day, Bellegarde, when he is in total possession of this beauty, is convinced that he could have found it in someone else who could have better accommodated his political ambition. Presently, he is accused of kidnapping and the entire court holds him in very low esteem. In fact, the queen mother obliges the king to declare himself against Bellegarde. The young baron is disgraced and is forbidden to return to court.

This unfortunate turn of events dispairs and depresses Bellegarde (now a marquis). The new Mme de Bellegarde, instead of attempting to understand her husband's ignominy and far from assuming the role of the prudent and sympathetic wife, wishes to remain "la maîtresse délicate." She confronts her husband about his melancholic state and his apparent disinterest in her. And as he is constantly persecuted by her verbal attacks at home, he begins to spend his time elsewhere.

Bellegarde attempts to regain the favor of His Majesty. When Charles IX dies and the new king is about to leave Poland, he is presented with an opportunity to do so:

Bellegarde voulut. . .se remettre en grâce auprés de Sa Majesté. On sçavoit par toute l'Europe que le Roi s'étoit dérobé de Pologne, & que le Senat étoit fort affligé de sa fuite. Bellegarde eut avis par un ami qu'il avoit à Venise que la Seigneurie qui étoit alliée avec la Pologne, & qui avoit interêt à maintenir cette alliance pour empêcher les progrez du Turc, faisoit dessein, si le nouveau Roi passoit par les Terres de Venise, de l'y retenir adroitement, jusqu'à ce que les députez de Pologne l'eussent atteint. Il jugea que ce seroit une rude ataque pour Sa Majesté, & que s'il pouvoit ou faire changer ce dessein, ou donner avis au Roi qu'il prît sa route par ailleurs, ce service effaceroit peut-être le souvenir passé. (p. 89)

The king grants him the rank of "Maréchal de France"; and indeed he is honored with so many distinctions that his new favor greatly surpasses his disgrace. This, nevertheless, proves insufficient to rekindle his love for his wife.

Mme de Bellegarde, perceiving that her husband's indifference has evolved into hatred, has the marquis surrounded by spies and is thus able to intercept several of the correspondences between the duc de Savoie and her husband. One letter in particular details the duke's plans (with Damville and other Italian princes) to negotiate peace by neutralizing the queen mother's influence. Out of spite for her husband, the marquise warns the queen. This latter employs Dugua in an attempt to rectify the situation.

Although the king does make Bellegarde Maréchal, he does it with such disdain that the new Maréchal suspects his wife of sabotaging his interests. He writes to the duchesse de Savoie so that she might uncover the truth--specifying that if Mme de Bellegarde is guilty, she is to be severely punished.

Mme de Bellegarde intercepts this message and petitions the queen mother for assistance. She confesses to the queen the indiscretions that love has forced her to commit. The queen confronts and reprimands Bellegarde for the mistreatment of his wife. The husband is rendered almost speechless and reponds only that he has chosen not to live with his wife because in the eyes of Rome, the marriage is not legitimate. Catherine promises to obtain the necessary dispensation.

As Mme de Bellegarde is an unusually beautiful woman, she attracts the attention of several gentlemen of the court including Bussi d'Amboise,

171

a favorite of Monsieur. The Marquis de Bellegarde perceives this infatuation with much delight; for although he is trying to prevent the queen from obtaining the necessary dispensation for his marriage, he is not at all optimistic about his chances of success. Thus he considers that an "intrigue de galanterie" would be a surer and more advantageous way of presenting a legitimate reason to divorce his wife.

Using one of his wife's attendants, he endeavors to cultivate this affair. Not only does he employ this servant to initiate his wife's interest in Bussi but he even attempts to make Bussi himself more infatuated with his wife by marveling at and extolling her qualities in his presence.

While Mme de Bellegarde is aware of Bussi's passion, she refuses him the opportunity to speak to her:

> Mais ses regards & ses actions (à lui) supléoient au default de sa langue, & n'étant pas satisfait de cette espece de langage, il (Bussi) voulut essayer si par ses lettres il pourroit se faire entendre plus intelligiblement. (p. 105)

Bussi employs this same attendant to advance his interests. The old lady, at the orders of Bellegarde, deceives Bussi into believing that Mme de Bellegarde is favorably receiving his propositions. These two conspirators receive the suitor's letters and even begin to fabricate responses in the name of the marquis' spouse.

Although the innocent Bussi is pleased with these tender albeit illegitimate responses, he very soon demands "de la bouche de la mareschelle" the assurance of his happiness. Everything is done to make him satisfied with less; but it is in vain, for he can now be content only with an "entretien particulier" with the object of his desire.

Bellegarde is determined to use his wife's adultery as a justification to dissolve the marriage, even if it means creating the appearance of an impropriety which does not in fact exist.

172

Hence, he plots to hire a servant of the duchesse de Nemours (a servant who resembles somewhat his wife) to impersonate her in a rendz-vous with Bussi. The imposter is notified of the time and place of this meeeting by means of a note that Mme de Bellegarde is able to intercept.

Thinking this rendez-vous to be a part of her husband's galanterie, Mme de Bellegarde decides to frustrate his efforts. Arriving at the designated garden one-half hour before the interview is to take place, she finds Bussi who, anticipating pleasures to come, thanks her for keeping her word and for granting this meeting. Mme de Bellegarde denies ever having made any such promises and assures Bussi that "on vous a trompé si on vous a fait tenir un autre *lang-age*" (emphasis added).

When the impostor arrives, she discovers Bussi and Mme de Bellegarde; and thinking the plot to be aborted, she alerts Bellegarde. He, on the contrary, interprets his wife's presence in the garden as a sign that she does in fact love Bussi and so decides to surprise the "lovers." To lend credence to his future accusations, he asks a witness (a certain Fervaques) to accompany him.

These two men, hidden in the foliage, overhear the last part of a long conversation where Mme de Bellegarde is discouraging Bussi's passion. Bellegarde is convinced, however, that his wife has been warned of his arrival in the garden and that previously she had "tenu des discours contraires à ceux-là." He reveals himself to his wife, claiming to have heard the entire conversation and advising Mme de Bellegarde of the futility of denying her passion at this point.

Mme de Bellegarde, assured of her own innocence, threatens to approach the queen mother with the counterfeit letters and the note arranging the impersonation. Bellegarde is speechless. Shortly thereafter, this incident is known to everyone. The queen mother ridicules Bellegarde in an insulting way. Monsieur incites all of the people attached to him against Bellegarde. But more than

173

all this, that which troubles the Maréchal the
most is that the dispensation is obtained from
Rome sanctioning his marriage.

Bellegarde can resolve neither to accept his
marriage nor to expose himself to the resentment
of the queen. He therefore leaves the court under
the pretext of going to Paris. Instead, he
withdraws for a second time to Piedmont--leaving
there only to capture the marquisate of Saluces
(Saluzzo). Consequently, this territory, cut off
from France, is taken over by the duc de Savoie;
and only with much toil and bloodshed can it be
recaptured.

NOUVELLES III AND IV

Part One

The story begins with a retrospective account of the intimate relationship between the Marquis d'Anglure and the duc de Guise. The duke's children and the marquis' son, Givry, shared the same tutors and the latter was accepted by the princes as though he were their brother. There appeared to be an eternal union between the two families.

Yet the League separates the duc de Guise from the interest of the king whereas the Marquis d'Anglure remains devoted to Henri III. Consequently, after the "Catastrophe des Etats de Blois," Givry d'Anglure finds himself the declared enemy of the very ones he had loved most.

Initially this divorce chagrins Givry enormously for he had sincerely esteemed the company of the *princes du sang* and had profoundly admired the budding charms of the princess their sister. But in addition to Henri III's attention and promises of future distinctions, it is the beauty and charm of a certain Mme de Maugiron that confirm the young Givry into the king's party.

This young and beautiful widow is one of the most striking "ornaments" of the court. And although Givry is only twenty-one, he has already surpassed by far most of his contemporaries. Before the age of eighteen, he had already completed his studies and his military training. He has a perfect knowledge of "des belles lettres" and mathematics and speaks Greek, Latin, and all the modern languages of Europe.

Givry and Mme de Maugiron fall madly in love. They spend entire days "en de douces conversations"; and whenever military duty interrupts these conversations, the beautiful

widow writes such tender letters to her lover that
they succeed in consoling him during her absence.

Givry always carry these letters with him in
a small case in which he keeps his most precious
possessions. He takes more care to insure the
safety of the letters than to insure his own.
Yet, in spite of his precautions, his case is
taken during an encounter with the enemy forces.
He is very sensitive to this loss; for in addition
to his personal loss, he is concerned that Mme de
Maugiron's stepchildren (who were in the League
party) might use them to the detriment of his
mistress' reputation.

He is in total despair when one day a
messenger from the duc de "Maine" (Mayenne)
returns the *cassette* containing his letters with
this explanation: the leaders of the League wish
not to enter into any "intrigue de galanterie" and
are therefore keeping only those papers pertaining
to the affairs of state.

When Givry isolates himself to re-read at
last his cherished letters, he is surprised to
find inscribed on the fold of each of them verses
of poetry in an unfamiliar handwriting. He won-
ders if the verses were written "au hasard" or if
they constitute "une censure judicieuse" of the
letters' content. As he examines the meaning of
the verses in light of the letters, he realizes
that these confessions of love by Mme de Maugiron
can be interpreted in a different way. The poems
point out the caprices of love and condemn the
excessive expressions of this passion.

With some reflection, Givry finds that he is
in total agreement with the poetic maxims. Now he
perceives Mme de Maugiron as a rather selfish and
unrealistic mistress; and during this moment of
reflection, he is persuaded that she is not the
only one capable of making him happy.

As Bellegarde is an intimate friend of Givry
and as the two of them never concealed anything
from each other, Givry recounts to his friend the
incident of his letters. Bellegarde hardly has
time to glance at the verse before he recognizes
the handwriting to be that of Mlle de Guise.

176

Since Givry had greatly admired Mlle de Guise when she was a child, he is very curious as to what she must be like as a young woman. He is equally curious about and inquires of Bellegarde of the "meaning" of the verses and whether or not they can be regarded as a "favor" with hopes of "d'heureux suites." Bellegarde counsels that his friend, if he truly loves Mme de Maugiron, should ignore the incident completely.

Conceding that he is in love with Mme de Maugiron, Givry maintains that he would not renounce an assured love for these verses whose meaning and purpose are not completely clear to him. Nevertheless, he feels that since he is young and since Mlle de Guise is one of the world's most beautiful princesses, he would be a fool not to pursue a possible affair with her. He is quite flattered by the thought that this great princess would consent to "correct" his love letters.

Upon returning to court, Givry learns that one of the prisoners-of-war held by the King of Navarre is a certain baron de Vins, one of the most faithful members of the Guise party. He seeks an interview with this prisoner to request news of the Guise household and especially of the princess. The baron informs Givry that the princess is more charming and more talented than any woman of her time and that he (Givry) has already seen the first attempts of her "talents" in several poems.

Assured that the princesse de Guise is indeed the mysterious poet, he inquires about the circumstances surrounding the composition of the verses:

Ne sçauriez-vous me dire ce qui obligea Mlle de Guise à les faire & s'ils ont été faits en particulier, ou en conversation generale. (p. 136)

The baron professes his ignorance on this matter as the princess had indicated to him only that she wanted to show the ladies of the court that those of the League surpassed them both in their "délicatesse de coeur" and in their "finesse d'esprit."

He suggests rather that Givry himself should go to ask Mlle de Guise her thoughts and intentions.

Bellegarde again advises his dear friend not to delude himself into thinking that he could have a love adventure with Mlle de Guise: first, he explains, she is a member of the enemy party and as no end to the war is in sight, he may never see her; secondly, she is of a noble family and will require a *prince du sang* for a husband. Givry is all too aware of this; yet he dreams incessantly of the princess and hardly thinks of Mme de Maugiron at all.

During the siege of Paris and other military campaigns, Givry shows many signs of his courage and the fate of the royal forces seems to rest on his shoulders. The King of Navarre, who admires Givry above all others, honors him with, among other distinctions, the government of Brie. He is hardly in possession of this function when he intercepts a shipment of wheat bound for Paris under a false passport. Recognizing the driver of this convoy to be a servant of the Guise family and upon learning from him that Mme de Guise and her daughter are in dire need of this shipment, Givry procures a legitimate passport and dispatches the provisions to Paris--consulting no other authority than his own passion.

This gesture is reported to the king who reacts violently; for the entire question of peace or war depends upon the fall or the resistance of this city. Through the intervention of Navarre, who explains to Henri Givry's sentimental reasons for such an unprofessional act, Givry receives only a reprimand from the king. It is to be the king's last act; for he is assassinated the following day.

Givry is grateful to Navarre and is one of the first to salute him as the King of France. In fact, Givry is so influential in getting others to do likewise that the new king owes the establishment and the tranquillity of the commencement of his reign to this officer. It is not that Henri de Navarre is not the rightful heir to the throne, but according to the law, his religion renders him ineligible. He is advised therefore to reconcile his right and his religion. A cease-fire is declared and negotiations begin.

During this truce, the king suggests that Givry travel to Paris to receive thanks for the assistance that he has provided for Mlle de Guise and her mother. Accompanied by his friend Belle-garde, he departs immediately.

Up to this point Givry has remained "decent" with Mme de Maugiron. He realizes well that he does not love her but he feels somewhat ashamed in betraying the hopes of this woman of whom he could not complain. She still writes him "par tous les courriers" and he answers promptly her every letter. But the sight of the princess destroys entirely the remaining traces of this con-sideration for Mme de Maugiron.

Before negotiations are finally broken off and the cease-fire ended by the duc de Maine (Mayenne) of the League Party, Givry has several interviews with Mlle de Guise but he does not declare his passion. He decides he needs more time to "faire éclater sa gloire." During these conversations, however, they speak often of Mme de Maugiron, and Givry assures the princess that her verses have dissipated the blindness of his heart concerning his mistress for whom he now feels only a faint indifference. Mlle de Guise is extremely pleased to learn of the effects of her poetry and has Givry repeat them to her at every possible occasion.

When the fighting recommences, all communi-cation with Paris is severed and Givry departs to confront the duc de Parme in battle. He retakes the city of Corbeil and sends the goods and pro-visions captured to Mlle de Guise with a message that there will be forthcoming shipments. The princess responds that she is accepting neither messages nor gifts from the enemy and that in spite of her "familiar" attitude during the cease-fire she is still Mlle de Guise and he Givry.

Givry is of course surprised by this reac-tion and can find nothing in his actions that could have provoked such harsh words. He attempts several times to appease her anger; but in spite

179

of his show of respect and zeal for her, she
remains "orgueilleusement *silente*." Givry spends
the entire winter sad and tormented; and to aug-
ment his chagrin, he receives every day bitter
reprimands from Mme de Maugiron.

As the king intends to lay siege to Rouen,
he recalls Givry from Brie. During this attack
Givry is dangerously wounded and the sadness which
possesses his soul augments the gravity of his
condition to such an extent that the doctors fear
for his life.

The king demands and receives an explanation
from his officer for his unusual depression.
Henri IV is touched by this predicament and promises to devise a plan to comfort him. The
Chevalier d'Oise (who knows Mlle de Guise well
through her uncle) has been taken prisoner. The
king agrees to free him provided he discovers what
Givry has done to displease Mlle de Guise and that
he report back this information.

PART TWO (NOUVELLE IV)

The Chevalier d'Oise faithfully and dili-
gently executes his commission and makes known
promptly to the king that Mlle de Guise complains
of a letter that Givry has written to her in which
he openly declares his love. As a princess, she
is greatly offended by the liberties that he has
taken; and were it not for Henri IV, she would
punish Givry with an immortal disdain ("mépris").
Instead, she promises the king to forgive this
trespass.

This promise of clemency comforts Givry
somewhat; but he is put in an equally perplexing
predicament: he has not written to Mlle de Guise
and can not think of why anyone else would forge
such a letter.

During most of the military activity that
follows--the duc de Parme forcing the king to

remove the siege from Rouen and the former's subsequent death at Caudebec--Givry is inactive and
requests to be transferred to his function at Brie
where he attempts to shed some light on his situation *vis à vis* Mlle de Guise. He is ultimately
afforded the opportunity to speak to her in person
and to deny authorship of the letter. This denial
sparks the princess' curiosity; she has the letter
shown to Givry. How surprised is he to learn that
this declaration of love is in the handwriting of
his dear friend Bellegarde!

Givry can not deny or complain about the
contents of the letter; it is instead Bellegard's
motives and the circumstances of its composition
that trouble him. In his search for Bellegarde to
demand an explanation, Givry finds him wounded yet
honored with a new distinction: the king has made
him "duc et pair." When finally confronted,
Bellegarde justifies his daring gesture as an act
of kindness on the part of a concerned friend. He
knows that Givry is uncertain as to Mlle de
Guise's sentiments; and persuaded that doubt is
the most painful of states, he undertook (he
contends) merely to clarify his friend's position.
If the princess has received this declaration
favorably, he continues, then Givry is truly
ungrateful for he should be happy. If, on the
other hand, she is irritated, Bellegarde has given
his friend the opportunity to deny honestly the
letter. Givry is convinced.

In the meantime, Mme de Maugiron has placed
so many spies around her lover that she learns of
his love for Mlle de Guise and of the incident of
the letter. In fact, she is so persistent and so
possessed with jealousy that she is able to discover the sentiments of her rival from the mouth
of the princess herself. She devises means to
eavesdrop on a conversation between Mlle de Guise
and one of her servants from which she learns that
the princess is more disposed to receive the
affections of Bellegarde than those of Givry.

This forsaken mistress, partly out of love
and partly out of jealousy, informs Givry of the
princesse de Guise's inclination and of
Bellegarde's betrayal. Unable to contain his emo-
tion, Givry embarks to confront his rival.

Henceforth, the relationship between the friends becomes increasingly strained and unfriendly until eventually the king has to be informed of their public rivalry. Henri uses the power and influence he has over Givry to calm this domestic disorder.

The people are tired of war; and as the duc de Maine has a particular interest in ending it, sincere negotiations are begun. During these negotiations, Givry is again able to see Mlle de Guise. They discuss the infamous letter. The princess confesses that "ce n' [est] pas l'écriture qui m'en [déplaît], c'[est] le sens" (p. 193). Givry now understands that the audacity that she finds so condemnable in him appears excusable in the case of his rival. This truth renders the hero speechless.

The king commands his subject and officer to live in peace with Bellegarde and promises that he will furnish him with so many opportunities to win the favor of the princess that she will forget Bellegarde. Conceding to the wishes of his king, Givry avoids all confrontations with his former friend.

The king's subsequent conversion and abjuration gain for him the affection and devotion of the people and permit him to enter triumphantly into Paris ("le roi fut à peine entré dans Paris que le calme s'y rétablit comme si jamais il n'y avoit eu de désordre"). Fulfilling his promise to provide Givry with every opportunity to serve the object of his desire, the king commands him to protect the Guise household. When Givry arrives to execute this order, he is well surprised to find that Bellegarde, with a company of volunteers, is already guarding the house.

The two officers experience such a bitter confrontation, even to the point of actual combat, that Mlle de Guise is obliged to intervene in person. Her intervention, however, merely confirms Givry's knowledge that Bellegarde is the perferred suitor (for all of her harsh admonitions are addressed specifically to the former).

The king, realizing the torments of love,

does all he can to console Givry and even goes so far as to speak to the princesse de Guise on his behalf. All is useless. As Bellegarde has led Mlle de Guise to believe that she could aspire to the throne itself, she barely conserves measures of civility with Givry.

This unfortunate suitor, whose passion is not destroyed, is afforded one last opportunity to converse with his beloved princess. But she is so severe that he perceives death as his only consolation. Seeking in effect every opportunity to receive this relief, Givry is wounded during the siege of Laon and expires a few days afterwards. As he knew beforehand his death to be imminent, he wrote a first and final letter to Mlle de Guise in which he explained his actions and sentiments. This letter is never delivered.

The king is so touched by this loss that he goes in person to complain to Mlle de Guise about her indifference and cruelty towards this great and irreplaceable man. The princess is affected neither by the death of the first nor the discourse of the second on his behalf.

Mme de Maugiron, on the other hand, falls into a depression that ends only with the end of her life. And while all of Paris resounds with shouts of joy for the absolution from Rome and for the reunion of all the factions in the kingdom, this woman dies pronouncing the name of her inconstant lover.

Maxime VI

La sensible delicatesse,
Suit toujoûrs pas à pas la sincere tendresse;
Il faut, pour aimer ardemment,
Ressentir delicatement
Tout ce qui part de ce qu'on aime;
Mais on tombe souvent, sur cela, dans l'erreur;
Et telle croit aller jusqu'au degré suprême
Des délicatesses du coeur,
Qui, si l'on se jugeoit severement soi-même,
Trouveroit que ce sont des caprices d'humeur.

Maxime VII

La Grande liberté dans les expressions
N'est pas toûjours l'effet des grandes passions.
On en reduit l'ardeur à des preuves frivoles,
Quand on la dissipe en paroles.
Il en est de l'amour, comme de la douleur.
Plus elle observe le silence,
Plus elle se renferme en secret dans un coeur,
Et plus elle a de violence.

Maxime VIII

Une influence dominante,
Oste au choix de nos coeurs leurs blâmes & Leur prix
Selon qu'elle est maligne ou bien-faisante,
D'un feu plus ou moins beau nous nous sentons (épris);
Heureuse en qui ce souverain caprice
Devient un acte de justice;
Heureux le coeur qui marchant au hazard,
Persuade au public que la raison le guide.
D'un si rare bonheur, c'est l'astre qui decide,
Et le discernement n'y prend aucune part.

Maxime IX

Quand, par d'heureux assortiments,
L'amour se trouve exemt de blâme,
Qu'on peut livrer toute son ame
A ses tendres ravissemens,
Il faut envisager le doux tems de la joie
Comme un moment qui fuit & qui ne revient plus,
Et compter pour perdu tout celui qu'on emploie
En des reproches superflus.

BIBLIOGRAPHY

WORKS BY MADAME DE VILLEDIEU

A) PROSE:

Alcidamie. 2 vol. Paris: Barbin, 1661

Lisandre, Nouvelle par Mlle des Jardins. Paris: Barbin, 1663.

Anaxandre, Nouvelle par Mlle des Jardins. Paris: Barbin, 1667.

Carmente, Histoire grecque par Mlle des Jardins. 2 vol. Paris: Barbin, 1667.

Cléonice, ou le Roman Galant. Paris: Barbin, 1669.

Le Journal Amoureux. 6 vol. Paris: Barbin, 1669-1671.

Annales Galantes. Paris: Barbin, 1670.

Mémoires du serail sous Amurat second. Paris: Barbin, 1670, 1673.

Les Amours des Grands Hommes. 4 vol. Paris: Barbin, 1671.

Les Exilés. 6 vol. Paris: Barbin, 1672, 1673.

Les Galanteries Grenadines. 2 vol. Paris: Barbin, 1673.

Mémoires de la vie d'Henriette Sylvie de Molière. 6 vol. Paris: Barbin, 1674.

Les Désordres de l'Amour. Paris: Barbin, 1675.

Les Nouvelles Afriquaines. Paris: Barbin, 1683.

Annales Galantes de Grèce. 2 vol. Paris: Barbin, 1687.

Portrait des Faiblesses Humaines. Paris: Barbin, 1685.

Oeuvres Complètes de Madame de Villedieu. 5 vol. Paris: Roslin Fils, 1741.

B) POETIC WORKS:

Le Carousel de Monseigneur le Dauphin. Paris: Barbin, 1662.

Recueil de Poésies de Mlle Desjardins. Paris: Barbin, 1662.

Recueil de Poésies de Mlle des Jardins augmenté de pluieurs pièces et Lettres en cette dernière édition. Paris: Barbin, 1664.

Fables ou Histoires Allégoriques, dédiées au Roy par Mme de Villedieu. Paris: Barbin, 1670.

C) DRAMATIC WORKS:

Manlius, Tragi-comédie par Mlle des Jardins. Paris: 1662.

Nitétis, Tragédie par Mlle des Jardins. Paris: Barbin, 1664.

Le Favory, Tragi-comédie par Mlle des Jardins. Paris: Billaine, 1665.

BIBLIOGRAPHY OF WORKS CITED

Arland, M. "Sur La Princesse de Clèves." Nouvelle Revue Française, 55 (1941), 603-609.

Barthes, Roland. *Essais Critiques.* Paris: Editions du Seuil, 1964.

----------. "Introduction à l'Art Structural du Récit." *Communications,* 8 (1966), 1-27.

_____. "Le Discours de l'Histoire. "*Social Science Information*, 6 (1967), 68-74.

Benveniste, Emil. *Problèmes de Linguistique Générale*. 2 vol. Paris: Gallimard, 1966, 1974.

Braudy, Leo. *Narrative Form in History and Fiction*. Princeton: University Press, 1970.

Chatenet, Henri. *Le Roman et les Romans d'une Femme de Lettres au XVIIe Siècle: Madame de Villedieu*. Paris: Champion, 1911.

Dallas, Dorothy. *Le Roman Français de 1660-1680*. *Paris: Gamber, 1932*.

Danto, Arthur C. *Analytical Philosophy of History*. Cambridge: The University Press, 1965.

Evans, Wilfred Hugo. *L'Historien Mézeray et la Conception de l'Histoire en France au XVIIe Siècle*. Paris: Gamber, 1930.

Francillon, Roger. *L'Oeuvre Romanesque de Madame de Lafayette*. Paris: Librairie José Corti, 1973.

Genette, Gérard. *Figures II, III*. Paris: Seuil, 1969, 1972.

Hipp, Marie-Thérèse. "Fiction & Réalité dans les Mémoires de la Vie de Henriette-Sylvie de *Molière* de Mme de Villedieu." *Le XVIIe Siècle*. 94-95 (1971), 93-117.

Jakobson, Roman. "Shifters, Verbal Categories, and the Russian Verb." *In Selected Writings*. vol II. Paris: Mouton, 1971.

Magne, Emil. *Madame de Villedieu*. Paris: Mercure de France, 1907.

Marguerite de Valois. *Mémoires*. In *Mémoires of the Court of Europe*. New York: P. F. Collier & Son, 1910, Vol. II.

May, George. "L'Histoire a-t-elle engendré le Roman?: Aspects Français de la question au seuil du siècle des Lumières." *RHLF*, 55 (1955), 155-176.

----------. *Le Dilemme du Roman au XVIIIe Siècle*. New Haven: Yale University Press, 1963.

Mézeray, F. Eudes de. *Histoire de France* contenant le règne du Roi Henri III et celui du Roi Henri IIII jusqu' à la Paix de Vervin inclusivement. Paris: Mathieu Guillemot, 1651. Vol. III.

----------. *Abrégé Chronologique ou extrait de* l'Histoire de France. Paris: Billaine, 1672. Vol. I, II.

Morrissette, Bruce. *The Life and Works of Marie-Catherine Desjardins: (Madame de Villedieu) 1632-1683*. St. Louis: Washington University Press, 1947.

Saint-Réal, C. Vichard, abbé de. *De l'Usage de* l'Histoire. In *Oeuvres Complètes*. Paris: 1745. Vol. II.

----------. *Dom Carlos, nouvelle historique*. In *Oeuvres Complètes*. Paris: Nyon, 1745. Vol. II.

Segrais, J-R. de. *Les Nouvelles Françoises ou les divertissemens de la Princesse Aurélie*. Paris: Huart, 1722. Vol. II.

Sévigné, Marquise de. *Lettres*. Ed. Gérard-Gailly. Paris: Gallimard, 1960, 1963.

Stierle, Karlheinz. "L'Histoire comme Exemple, l'Exemple comme Histoire." *Poétique*, 10 (1972), 176-198.

Villedieu, Madame de. *Les Désordres de l'Amour*. Ed. M. Cuénin. Paris: Droz, 1970.

Valincourt, Jean Baptiste de Trousset. *Lettres à la Marquise sur le sujet de la Princesse de Clèves*. Paris: Mabre-Cramoisy, 1678.

190

Woshinsky, Barbara R. *La Princesse de Clèves*:
The Tension of Elegance. The Hague:
Mouton, 1973.

BIBLIOGRAPHY OF WORKS CONSULTED

A) NOVELS, NOUVELLES AND OTHER WORKS OF
THE SEVENTEENTH CENTURY

Anselme, Pierre Guibours de Sainte-Marie.
*Histoire de la Maison Royale de France et
des Grands Officiers de la Couronne*. 2
vol. Paris: Loyson, 1674.

Boursault, E. *Le Prince de Condé, nouvelle historique*. Paris: Didot, 1792.

Brantôme, P. de Bourdeilles. *Mémoires*. . .
*contenans les vies des hommes illustres et
grands capitaines français*. Leyde: Sambix
le Jeune, 1665. Vol. III.

----------. *Mémoires*. . .*contenans les vie des
dames illustres de son temps*. 2 vol.
Leyde: Sambix le Jeune, 1666.

Bussi-Rabutin, R. de. *Histoire Amoureuse des
Gaules*. Revue et annotée par P. Boiteau,
*suivie des romans historico-satiriques du
XVIIe siècle recueillis et annotés par C.
Livet*. Paris: Jannet, 1656.

Chiverni, Phillipe Hurault (comte de). *Mémoires
d'Etat*. Paris: Billaine, 1636.

Corneille, Pierre. *Oeuvres Complètes*. Ed. A.
Stegmann. Paris: Seuil, 1963.

Descartes, René. *Discours de la Méthode pour bien
conduire sa raison et chercher la vérité
dans les sciences*. Ed. Mlle. Barthélemy.
Paris: Bibliothèque de Cluny, 1943.

Du Plaisir. *La Duchesse d'Estramène*. Paris:
Blageart, 1682.

----------. *Sentiments sur les Lettres et sur
l'Histoire avec des scrupules sur le stile*.
Paris: Blageart and Quinet, 1683.

191

Gomberville, M. le Roy de. *Polexandre.* 5 vols.
Paris: Courbé, 1641.

Guilleragues, G. de. *Lettres Portugaises,
Valentins, et Autres Oeuvres.* Ed. F.
Deloffre. Paris: Garnier, 1962.

*Histoire des Amours du Grand Alcandre, ou sous des
noms d'emprunt se lisent les aventures amou-
reuses d'un grand prince du dernier siècle.*
Paris: Guillemot, 1652.

La Calprenède, G. de Coste de. *Cassandre.* Paris:
de Sommaville, 1644-1647. Vol. I, II.

Lafayette, Madame de. *Romans et Nouvelles.* Ed.
E. Magne. Paris: Garnier, 1961.

----------. *Vie de la Princesse d'Angleterre.* Ed.
Marie-Thérèse Hipp. Geneva: Droz, 1967.

----------. Correspondance. Ed. A. Beaunier.
Paris: Gallimard, 1942. Vol. I.

----------. *La Princesse de Clèves.* Ed. Louise
Vilmorin. Paris: éditions Gallimard et
Librairie Générale Française, 1958.

La Mothe Le Vayer, François de. *Discours de
l'Histoire.* Paris: J. Camusat, 1638.

----------. *Du peu de certitude qu'il y a dans
l'Histoire.* Paris: n.p., 1668.

Le Moyne, Pierre. *De l'Histoire.* Paris: Mabré-
Cramoisy, 1670.

La Rochefoucauld, François de. *Oeuvres Complètes.*
Ed. Martin-Chauffier, et al. Paris:
Bibliothèque de la Pléiade. Editions
Gallimard, 1964.

Pascal, Blaise. *Pensées.* Ed. Ch-M des Granges.
Paris: Garnier Frères, 1964.

Scarron, P. Le Roman Comique. In *Romanciers du
XVIIe Siècle.* Paris: Gallimard, 1958.

Scudéry, M. de. *Artamène, ou le Grand Cyrus.*
Paris: Courbé, 1650-1653.

Segrais, J-R. de. *Les Nouvelles Françoises ou les divertissemens de la Princesse Aurélie.* Paris: Huart, 1722. Vol. II.

Sorel, Charles. *Les Nouvelles Choisies ou se trouve divers accidens d'Amour et de Fortune.* Paris: David, 1645. Vol. II.

----------. *De la Connoissance des bons livres, ou examen de plusieurs auteurs.* Paris: n.p., 1671.

Urfé, H. d'. *l'Astrée,* preceded by *Le Serpent dans la Bergerie* by G. Genette. Paris: Union Générale d'Editions, 1964.

B) CRITICAL WORKS CONSULTED

Adam, Antoine. *Histoire de la Littérature Française au XVIIe Siècle.* 5 vol. Paris: del Duca, 1949-1956.

Ashton, H. *Madame de Lafayette, sa vie et ses oeuvres.* Cambridge: University Press, 1932.

Baldner, R. W. *Bibliography of Seventeenth-Century French Prose Fiction.* New York: Columbia University Press, 1967.

----------. "Aspects of the 'nouvelle' in France between 1600 and 1660." *Modern Language Quarterly,* December 1961, 351-357.

Bar, Francis. *Le Genre Burlesque en France au XVIIe Siècle: Etude de Style.* Paris: Editions d'Artrey, 1960.

Beaunier, A. *L'Amie de La Rochefoucauld.* Paris: Flammarion, 1927.

Bénichou, Paul. *Morales du Grand Siècle.* Paris: Gallimard, 1948.

Booth, Wayne C. *The Rhetoric of Fiction.* Chicago: The University Press, 1961.

Bray, Bernard. *L'Art de la Lettre Amoureuse des Manuels aux Romans:* 1550-1700. Paris: Mouton, 1967.

Bray, René. *La Formation de la Doctrine Classique en France*. Paris: Hachette, 1927.

Burks, Arthur W. "Icon, Index, and Symbol." *Philosophy and Phenomenological Research,* 9 (1949), 673-689.

Cioranescu, Alexandre. *Bibliographie de la Littérature Française du Dix-Septième Siècle*. 3 vol. Paris: Editions du Centre National de la Recherche Scientifique, 1965.

Chamard, H. and G. Rudler. "Les Sources Historiques de *La Princesse de Clèves*." *Revue du Seizième Siècle*, 2 (1914), 92-131, 289-321; 5 (1917-18), 1-20, 231-243.

Chavardès, Maurice. *Histoire de la Librairie en France*. Paris: P. Walleffe, 1967.

Cherbuliez, V. "L'Ame Généreuse: *La Princesse de Clèves*." *Revue des Deux Mondes,* 15 March 1910, 274-298.

Chomsky, N. *Aspects of the Theory of Syntax*. Cambridge: The M.I.T. Press, 1965.

Collingwood, R. G. *The Idea of History*. Ed. T. M. Knox. London: The Clarendon Press, 1948.

Coulet, H. *Le Roman Français jusqu'à la Révolution*. 2 vol. Paris: Colin, 1967-68.

----------. "Un Siècle, un Genre." *RHLF*, 3-4 (mai-juin 1977), 359-373.

Croce, B. *History--Its Theory and Practice*. Trans. D. Ainslee. New York, 1960.

Cuénin, M. "La Terreur sans la Pitié: 'La Comtesse de Tende.'" *RHLF*, 3-4 (mai-juin 1977), 478-500.

Danaby, Michael. "Le Roman est-il chose femelle?" *Poétique,* 25 (1976), p. 85.

194

Daspré, A. "Le Roman Historique et l'Histoire."
   RHLF, 2-3 (mars-juin 1975) 235-245.

Dédéyan, Charles. *Madame de Lafayette.* Paris:
   Société d'Edition d'Enseignement Supérieur,
   1965.

Delhez-Sarlet, C. "Style Indirect Libre et 'Point
   de vue' dans *La Princesse de Clèves.*
   Cahiers d'Analyse Textuelle, 6 (1964),
   70-80.

Deloffre, F. *La Nouvelle en France à l'Age
   Classique.* Paris: Didier, 1967.

Démoris, René. *Le Roman à la Première Personne.*
   Paris: Librairie Armand Colin, 1975.

----------. "De l'Usage du Nom Propre dans le
   Roman Historique." *RHLF*, 2-3 (mars-juin
   1975), 268-289.

Doubrovsky, Serge. *Corneille et la Dialectique
   du Héros.* Paris: Gallimard, 1963.

Duchene, R. "Signification du Romanesque: l'
   Exemple de Madame de Sévigné." *RHLF*, 3-4
   (mai-août 1977), 578-595.

Duchet, Cl. "L'Illusion Historique" l'Enseignement des Préfaces (1815-1832)." *RHLF*, 2-3
   (mars-juin 1975), 245-268.

Dulong, Gustave. *L'Abbé de Saint-Réal: Etude sur
   les Rapports de l'Histoire et du Roman au
   XVIIe Siècle.* Paris: Champion, 1921.

Durry, M-J. "Le Monologue Interieur dans *La Princesse de Clèves.*" In *La Littérature Narrative d'Imagination.* Paris: Presses Uni-
   versitaires de France, 1959, 86-93.

Elliot, J. H. *Europe Divided 1559-1598.* In *History of Europe.* Ed. J. H. Plumb. New York:
   Harper & Row, 1968.

Fabre, Jean. "L'Art de l'Analyse dans *La Prin-
   cesse de Clèves.*" *Publications de la
   Faculté des Lettres de l'Université de
   Strasbourg,* Fascicule 105 (1946), 261-301.

Friedman, Norman. *Form and Meaning in Fiction.*
Athens: The University of Georgia Press,
1975.

Fumaroli, Marc. "Les Mémoires du XVIIe Siècle au
Carrefour des Genres." *Le XVIIe Siècle,*
94-95 (1971), 7-37.

Garavini, F. "L'Itinéraire de Sorel: du *Francion
à la Science Universelle.*" *RHLF,* 3-4 (mai-
juin 1977), 432-440.

Godenne, René. "L'Association 'nouvelle-petit
roman' entre 1650 et 1750." *Cahiers de
l'Association Internationale des Etudes
Françaises,* 18 (1966), 67-78

----------. "Un Plagiaire de Segrais au XVIIe
Siècle." *Le XVIIe Siècle,* 79 (1968),
95-104.

----------. "Comment appeler un auteur de
nouvelle?" *Romantic Review,* 58 (1967),
38-43.

----------. *Histoire de la Nouvelle Française aux
XVIIe et XVIIIe Siècles.* Geneva: Droz,
1970.

Green, F. C. "The Critic of the seventeenth-
century and his attitude towards the French
novel." *Modern Philology,* 1926-27, 285-295.

Hainsworth, George. *Les 'Nouvelas Exemplaires' de
Cervantes en France au XVIIe Siècle: Con-
tribution à l'étude de la nouvelle en
France.* Paris: Champion, 1933.

Henein, E. "Les Nouvelles de Camus et les
'Agencements.'" *RHLF,* 3-4 (mai-août 1977),
440-459.

Hepp, N. "La Belle et la Bête, ou la Femme et le
Pédant dans l'Univers Romanesque du XVIIe
Siècle." *RHLF,* 3-4 (mai-août 1977),
564-578.

Hipp, Marie-Thérèse. "Quelques Formes du Discours Romanesque chez Madame de Lafayette et chez Mademoiselle Bernard." *RHLF*, 3-4 (mai-août 1977), 507-523.

Hourcade, P. "La Représentation de la Femme dans 'La Précieuse.'" *RHLF*, 3-4 (mai-août 1977), 470-478.

Jones, Shirley, "Examples of Sensibility in the late Seventeenth-century Novel in France." *Modern Language Review*, 1966, 199-208.

Kaps, H-K. *Moral Perspectives in La Princesse de Clèves*. Eugene: The University of Oregon Books, 1968.

Kassai, G. "Indirect dans *La Princesse de Clèves*." *Les Lettres Nouvelles*, mai-juin 1970, 123-132.

Laugaa, Maurice. *Lectures de Mme de Lafayette*. Paris: Colin, 1971.

Lotringer, S. "La Structuration Romanesque." *Critique*, 277 (1970), p. 106.

Macksey, R. and E. Donato ed. *The Structuralist Controversy: The Languages of Criticism and the Sciences of Man*. Baltimore: The John Hopkins University Press, 1972.

Magendie, M. *Le Roman Français au XVIIe Siècle, de l'Astrée au Grand Cyrus*. Paris: Droz, 1932.

Magne, E. *Le Coeur et l'Esprit de Mme de Lafayette*. Paris: Emile-Paul frères, 1927.

Marin, Louis. "Remarques Critiques sur l'Enonciation: La Question du présent dans le discours." *MLN*, 95/5 (October 1976), 913-939.

Martin, H. J. *Livre, Pouvoir et Société à Paris au XVIIe Siècle*. Paris: Droz, 1969. Vol. II.

Molino, Jean. "Qu'est-ce que le Roman Historique." *RHLF*, 2-3 (mars-juin 1975), 195-235.

Mornet, D. "Les Enseignements des Bibliothèques Privées, 1750-80. *RHLF*, 16 (1910), 449-496.

Ranum, Orest. "Introduction" to Bossuet's *Discourse on Universal History*. Chicago: University of Chicago Press, 1976.

----------. *National Consciousness, History, and Political Culture in Early Modern Europe*. Baltimore: The Johns Hopkins Press, 1975.

Ratner, M. *Theory and Criticism of the Novel in France from 'Astrée to 1750*. New York: n.p., 1937.

Raynal, M.-A "Introduction" to *Anthropologie de la Nouvelle Française*. Lausanne: La Guilde du Livre, 1950.

----------. *Le Talent de Madame de Lafayette*. Paris: Picart, 1927.

Reed, Gervais E. *Claude Barbin, Libraire de Paris sous le Règne de Louis XIV*. Paris: Centre de Recherches d'Histoire et de Philologie. Section IV de l'Ecole Pratique des Hautes Etudes: Histoire et Civilisation du livre, 5, 1974.

Rogolot, François: "Emergence du Nom Propre dans la Nouvelle: Des Periers, Onomaturge." *MLN*, 92 no. 4 (May 1977), 676-690.

Rolfe, F. P. "On the Bibliography of the seventeenth-century novel." *PMLA*, 1934, 1071-1086.

Rouben, C. "Histoire et Géographie Galantes au Grand Siècle: *Histoire Amoureuse des Gaules* et la *Carte du Pays de Braquerie* de Bussi-Rabutin." *Le XVIIe Siècle*, 93 (1971), 55-73.

Rousset, Jean. *Forme et Signification*. Paris: Corti, 1963, pp. 17-45.

Roy, C. "Le Roman d'Analyse." *La Nef*, 30 (1959), 61-66.

Salmon, John H. M. *Society in Crisis: France in the Sixteenth Century*. New York: St. Martin's Press, 1975.

Steiner, A. "A French Poetics of the Novel in 1683." *Romantic Review*, 30 (1939), 235-243.

Terrebasse, Henri de. *Histoire et Généalogie de la Maison de Maugiron en Viennois*. Lyon, 1905.

Turnell, M. *The Novel in France*. London: H. Hamilton, 1950.

Varga, K. "Pour une Définition de la Nouvelle à l'Epoque Classique." *Cahiers de l'Association Internationale des Etudes*. 18 (1966), 53-65.

Weinrich, Harold. *Le Temps*. trans. by Michele Lacoste. Paris: Editions du Seuil, 1973.

Williams, R. C. *Bibliography of the Seventeenth-Century Novel*. New York: n.p., 1931.

Zeller, Sister Mary-Francine. *New Aspects of Style in the Maxims of La Rochefoucauld*. Washington: The Catholic University Press, 1954.